MW01254534

Not one credit card company, bank or private lender ... ...e *Wealth Mechanic* programme. Major lending organisations would be on their knees before they knew what hit them, should their customers discover and act on Max Eames' *dynamite* debt wipe-out system.

Captured between the covers is the most rapidly powerful and self-sustaining financial recovery method for ANY individual, private enterprise, or business concern – use it to *get* out of debt, *stay* out of debt and build up reserves of surplus cash.

I advise EVERY person who struggles with debt – small, medium or large – to cancel everything in your diaries, and not only read but ACT ON this book… starting this minute. You'll never again be financially beholden to anyone, and one day you'll laugh when you look back at the years 'in the red', not knowing how *simple* it was to get out. Start to enjoy your new 100% debt-free life today.

Paul F Gorman,
author of *The Game of Business*

Whenever you're playing to win in life, an inspirational coach never fails to accelerate the game-plan. Max Eames is most definitely the man to have on your side when you're *determined* to finish on top. By combining powerful strategies with proven techniques, Max motivates you to be the best you can be and won't let you settle for less than you deserve.

Kyran Bracken MBE,
motivational speaker, 2003 Rugby World Cup Winner,
and author of *Beyond The Scrum*

Whether you aspire to improve your personal finances or to put your business accounts on firmer footing, the stories and case studies in the *Wealth Mechanic* programme bring the breakthrough strategies to life. Max Eames's insight and understanding skillfully inform each and every page of this step-by-step methodology, aimed squarely at those of us who are committed to making success-stories of our personal, professional and financial lives.

Brian James,
management consultant and author of
Don't Work for Your Business – Make Your Business Work for You

The *Wealth Mechanic* is a gift; an invitation to emerge from debt and take control of your financial future. Brilliant in its simplicity, it's packed from start to finish with sound principles, insights and techniques. Max Eames has an ability to view personal struggle through the eyes of wisdom, imagination and warmth. Every page is a call to arms, with immediately practical guidelines for concentrating your thoughts and emotions, and an incentive to more fully embrace the things that money can't buy.

Joel Rothschild,
author of *Signals* and *Hope*

under
the hood

PRAISE FOR 'UNDER THE HOOD'

If you're struggling with some of the practicalities in life – money, relationships, your job or your health – *Under the Hood* is essential reading. Max Eames's turnaround from a slow but steady financial meltdown reminds you of the price of your own limited thinking... especially when it's buried beneath the surface. Understand the Galatea Effect so it works *for* you, not against you – in the right hands, it's a powerful tool that *you* can use to master your own destiny.

Sheila Steptoe,
author of *Master Your Own Destiny*

Under the Hood allows the simple psychology of the Galatea Effect to unfold before your very eyes. Max Eames, a psychotherapist with powerful spiritual vision, reminds us of the opportunity we all have within us: to recognise our conflicting beliefs before awakening the inner power to make long-lasting change. Start to reclaim the promising future you've *deserved* all along.

Tracey Ash,
author of *Life Vision: Awakening Your Power Within*

Recalibrate your relationship with money, your career, your family and friends, and ultimately *yourself*: understand and apply the principles of the Galatea Effect. *Under the Hood* gets right to the nuts and bolts of our personal psychology, penetrating layers of fear, of mental habits and conditioning, and of self-judgment.

Pippa Merivale,
author of *Follow Your Yellow Brick Road*

Under the Hood offers a uniquely practical exploration of the unconscious self through the eyes of an experienced psychotherapist. Use Max Eames's simple but profound insights to finally understand the link between our thinking, our behaviour and the futures we create. The Galatea Effect is undeniable proof that our intentions, prayers and thoughts can – and do – affect our physical reality.

June-Elleni Laine,
author of *Mandala: The Art of Creating Future*

Under the Hood reveals the mystery of the Galatea Effect so that you can understand the tricky relationship between unconscious thoughts and the money in your wallet. Use it to transform your bank balance, and then apply it to the rest of your life. Max Eames uses accessible psychology and everyday language, exploring with wisdom the profound effect of our fear-based thoughts and emotions.

Becky Walsh,
author of *Living Without Fear*

under
the hood

Secret strategies YOU can use
to 'recalibrate' inner beliefs
and put MORE MONEY
in your pocket...
starting today

NORTH STAR

Max Eames

AUTHOR OF 'WEALTH MECHANIC'
ILLUSTRATED BY RACHELLE LALANDE

10 9 8 7 6 5 4 3 2

First published in the United Kingdom by
North Star Press Ltd, 212 Piccadilly, London W1J 9HG
www.northstarpress.co.uk

A division of
North Star Group Ltd, 212 Piccadilly, London W1J 9HG

www.northstargroup.com

A CIP catalogue record is available for this book from the British Library.

ISBN: 978-0-9553629-4-1

    1. Personal Finance 2. Success – Psychological Aspects

Layout by SBCreative (info@sbcreative.org)

Printed and bound in the United States and the United Kingdom by
Lightning Source Inc/Lightning Source Ltd
USA: 1246 Heil Quaker Blvd, La Vergne, TN 37086
UK: Chapter House, Pitfield, Kiln Farm, Milton Keynes MK11 3LW

To Lisa – I will always value the depth of our conversations, the breadth of our shared thinking, and the resilience you showed during what was a soul-searching process

ACKNOWLEDGEMENTS

Nobody writes a book in isolation. The process is a rich one that ultimately involves more people than I could ever have imagined. I'd like to thank the people whose names stand out, but also to express my gratitude to those who, often in a quieter way, supported the writing as it developed.

I am most grateful for the generosity and creativity of Rachelle Lalande, whose unique humour comes through the illustrations, and has brought this work to life. The same holds true for Shelley Bray, Lisa Blann and Cliona McGrogan, whose professional approach to the book's layout gave shape and focus to the finished product.

There is a school of thought that says you can't heal anybody until you heal yourself. I've definitely been through the process of losing my way then finding it again, and without a handful of individuals as guides I would never have taken myself down this particular journey.

I owe much to my mentors: Joe Bailey, Ray Deutsch, Paul Gorman, Suzanna McInerney, Ana-Amalia Ruccio, Brian Smith, Lesley Standen and Josephine Van Schaick. From time to time, each of us is called upon to illuminate the path of another... and their light has helped me to more fully discover my own.

A great deal is owed to Dennis Williams for streamlining my life at the beginning of this project so that I was shielded from the day's distractions. His *manaakitanga* and his continued resolve that I should pursue my calling have been much-appreciated gifts.

Much is also owed to my parents, who gave me every possible resource I would need to succeed in life – I just wish I had been willing or able to learn the lessons earlier in the game. I thank them for all they have done, and for believing in me… even when I did things that were 'unbelievable' in their eyes.

To my sisters and my grandparents I owe a great deal, for they were a big part of shaping the person I am today.

My gratitude goes out to those who read this book or otherwise inspired me while it was a stack of papers in a ring binder – their critical eye, encouragement, wisdom, and practical advice were much appreciated: Gerhard Boomgaarden, Donald Eames, Paul Gorman, Alexa Hodgson, Brian James, Bruce Jones, Logan Lewis-Proudlock, Chris Lynch, Trish Miller, Jennifer Pegg, Joel Rothschild, Debbie Shimadry, Lesley Standen, and Brian Stones. Lending particular and essential expertise in giving shape to this project throughout its early stages, I doff my hat to Lisa Howard and Paul Holder.

I owe a great deal to the people who inspired and shaped my thinking as a psychotherapist. It has been a privilege to be a guide on their particular journey whilst they guided me on mine. In particular, I would like to thank my clients, who obviously can't be named, but who have challenged and consolidated my thinking with each hour we've spent working together.

Much is owed to the handful of friends and family who have passed away. Their humour, their creativity and their inspiration will not be forgotten.

And to those who have in one way or another played a part in keeping me both grounded and inspired within what has been a difficult journey, I am deeply grateful: Erhan Baki, Carol Bentley, Eleanor Braterman, Odile Brennan, Christine Bryon, John Bunk, Dennis Carney, Dan Castle, Jonathan Clark, Chantal Cooke, Marita Crawley, Reg de Roche, Stella Duffy, Morgan Evans, Anupam Ganguli, Mindy Gibbins-Klein, David Graham, Pam Graham, Susie Greenwood, Stephen Harvison, Diana Heller, Paul Holder, Alfred Hurst, June-Elleni Laine, Kris Lebrooy, Wendy Lefort, Betty Leigh, Ann Maurice, John McCormack, Deano McCullogh, Barbara Meiklejohn-Free, Pippa Merivale, Ollie Muncaster, Tim Muncaster, Dee Parsons, Yashwant Patel, Kayt Raymond, Ed Rivis, Amanda Roberts, Gaynor Roberts, Tina Robinson, Paul Ross, Carla Shehfe, Debbie Shimadry, Sabina Spencer, Linda Stacey, Lesley Standen, Janis Stanford, Sheila Steptoe, Caroline Stanley, Julia Stephenson, Denise Stones, Cathriona Sullivan, Chris Taylor, Penny Thompson, Elaine Tulloch, Nick Williams and Hollie Wilson.

CONTENTS

INTRODUCTION

Discover Why So Many Of Us Drive With The Needle On Empty

CHAPTER 1

CHAPTER 2

CHAPTER 3

When Warning Lights Flash, Pull Over And Peek Under The Hood

CHAPTER 4

CHAPTER 5

CHAPTER 6

Before Setting Off Again, Have A Look In The Rear-View Mirror

CHAPTER 7

CHAPTER 8

CHAPTER 9

Decide What You *Really* Mean
By Prosperity, Freedom And Abundance

CHAPTER 10

CHAPTER 11

CHAPTER 12

INTRODUCTION
If You're In Debt, Welcome To The Fraternity

In the late 1980s, I moved from the USA to Britain and began my career as an architect. After five years of a student lifestyle, I felt as if I had somehow *arrived*. Within the first week of my new job, I opened a bank account with a four-figure overdraft. I convinced myself that the good life had just begun. A young man in my twenties, I finally had money to burn. And burn it I did. I later discovered that I was spending more than £20 a day (and that's roughly $40) on fripperies without even giving it a moment's thought.

When changes to my work contract meant things took a turn for the worse, my back was completely against the wall. Prior to that stage, I'd managed for years to keep all the balls in the air, but the inevitable consequence of my behaviour hit me like a sledgehammer. My life abruptly became one of worry, sleepless nights, self-recrimination, and boring weekends spent home alone.

All those bills – *numbers* endlessly swimming around in my head. I didn't yet know the exact figures, but I was down by tens of thousands.

A defining moment came when I had to sell my prized possession – my beloved blue scooter – in order to pay my rent. As if that weren't enough, my change in circumstances alienated a few 'friends' along the way. Some of them stuck it out through my difficult patch, but a lot of them went the way of my self-esteem, my self-belief, and my self-respect.

The average client under the age of 25 who sought the advice of the UK's Consumer Credit Counselling Service owed £15,000 according to a report issued 12 September 2005. But it seemed that American 'twenty-somethings' fared little better, according to an August 2006 analysis of credit records conducted by Experian. With the average debt up 10 per cent to $16,120, many were found to be changing career plans in order to service their debts.

1

Still young enough to get my European National Rail Pass, I was thinking of jumping on the tracks instead. Luckily I discovered another way out. Instead of getting a handle on my situation, I first tried to borrow money from a relative – but the biggest gift I ever received was that he turned me down. Eventually I decided to save my *own* skin by developing what evolved into the Wealth Mechanic programme (the combination of mindset and strategy that inspired this book and its companion, *Fix Your Finances*), and clawed my way back to financial equilibrium.

It was perhaps my fate to learn the lessons the hard way: fellowship programmes… hypnosis… life coaching… group chanting… you name it; I rode the ride and bought the T-shirt. Along the way, I've gained a lot of insight into what leads us toward destructive overspending, having struggled for years with my own obsessive thought-patterns, compulsive behaviours, and self-esteem issues.

In America, a National Consumer Law Centre report on 27 November 2007 cited Federal Reserve household debt figures of some $730 billion from credit cards alone. Meanwhile, debts taken on by British families have overtaken the size of the nation's economy. People have borrowed so much that as of the start of 2006, total debt outstripped the UK's gross domestic product, according to the 13 February 2006 Telegraph.

I was able to give shape to these experiences through the rigour of training as a psychotherapist. Today I specialise in the psychology of fast-track financial freedom and 100% proven debt-elimination strategies. It probably comes as no surprise that the driving force for taking this path was a passion for understanding the behaviours and beliefs that had been making my own life such a roller-coaster ride. The Wealth Mechanic programme is thus a culmination of my experiences and the experiences of others. It has evolved over the years into a systematic approach, one bringing positive changes to the lives of many – and it could well change *your* life too.

There Really *Is* 'Life After Debt'

Believe it or not, there really *is* such a thing as 'life after debt', and within these pages you'll find this out for yourself. Like me, *you'll* rediscover some long-lost dreams – and you'll map out a way to make a lot of them come true.

I'm guessing you bought this book because you saw yourself, or someone you care about, struggling with the burden of debt. But there's something more important. You don't *just* want to be free of your debts. Whether or not you're willing to admit it to yourself, you'd like life to be a little bit more exciting – you'd like to create *wealth* for yourself at the same time. And by combining the right mindset and strategy, you can eventually achieve *that*, too.

You may be wondering: how much time would I need to devote to the Wealth Mechanic programme each week? We all lead busy lives, and for a book to do more than just sit on the shelf, what the author invites you to do has to fit in with the rest of your daily routine. So here's the answer: you really *can* demolish decades of debt – and it should take you less time than you spend *eating breakfast* each day.

At Last: A Genuine Opportunity For A Fresh Start

The Wealth Mechanic programme requires nothing more than the money you've already got in your pocket. It's a simple re-focus of your present income – making it work *for* you instead of against you.

But what makes the particular approach that inspired this book *different*? A number of factors place the Wealth Mechanic's 'financial fix-it formula' head and shoulders above much of what you might have seen or heard about elsewhere:

- You don't need to be making a lot of money

- You don't need the willpower of a Buddhist monk

- You can apply the simple tips and techniques without having to learn all about finances

- You can launch your personal success strategy after an hour or two of groundwork

Maybe you *too* are ready for a fresh start. So, what would you have achieved at the end of the Wealth Mechanic programme? You'd be free from debt forever, right? Yes, but that's not all by any means. Unlike many money-management strategies, the programme helps you understand how and why you got into debt, so you can be sure to avoid doing it again in the future. And this essential understanding of your own particular brand of 'personal psychology' is the focus of the book you hold in your hands right now.

After all, perhaps the biggest gift you could give yourself would be the opportunity for a fresh start, a chance to repair the engine and calibrate it to your own specifications. *Under The Hood* provides you with the possibility of creating an entirely new vision of your future, and then underpins it with simple but powerful psychology that will propel you toward it in the quickest possible time.

The Secret Science Of The Galatea Effect

A bit of magic was most certainly involved in the ancient myth that characterises the principle we'll be using throughout this book – but who doesn't believe in magic? The story goes that a Cypriot prince named Pygmalion set out to commission an ivory statue of the ideal woman. The result was so beautiful that he fell in love with the statue itself – and even worse, he actually *named* it: Galatea. Every day he prayed to the goddess

Venus, asking her to bring Galatea to life. Venus eventually granted his wish, and the couple lived happily ever after.

Don't ever underestimate the power of self-expectation. More commonly known as a self-fulfilling prophecy, we psychotherapists had to get fancy and call it the Galatea Effect. For each and every one of us, what we expect to come true in our mind's eye has a tendency to come true in reality.

So how can *you* take advantage of the Galatea Effect? Instead of considering a present lack of wealth as evidence that you're somehow 'meant to be poor', you might want to take responsibility for that aspect of your overall belief system – and then set out to change it, once and for all.

The book is intentionally divided into brief stand-alone sections. You needn't start off by reading the contents from cover to cover. You may firstly be tempted to skip around, dip your toes in certain sections, look at a couple of the self-guided tests, and seek out the parts you think are most relevant to your situation. That's fine, but after you've finished, promise me you'll go back and read the book from start to finish. This information is at its most powerful when you understand how the concepts and strategies fit together in sequence.

But it's not enough just to *read* this book. *Action* is what counts. Never feel guilty about writing in the margins of a paperback. Good books are tools; you're meant to scratch them up.

Scribble your notes in red pen. Use different colours. I write down anything I want to take action on. I draw pictures in the margins. And I jot down the pages of material I don't yet understand, or that I want to revisit. My favourite books look as if they've been run over by a bus by the time I turn to the final page. To me, that's the sign of a very good book!

No Need To Get Your Hands Greasy

At a recent one-day workshop, a participant made a comment about the Wealth Mechanic programme that was probably true for three-quarters of the room. 'But I don't want to get my hands greasy!' said a wonderfully boisterous lady from the back of the room. 'And I don't want to know *anything* about fixing cars! Why on earth do you call this programme The Wealth *Mechanic*?'

'It's just a metaphor,' I reminded her. 'Hardly anyone wants to look under the hood, but that's the whole point: you do want to know EVERYTHING about fixing your personal finances.'

So if you're cash-strapped month after month, *Under The Hood* is where you'll discover whether or not your struggle with money has more to do with what's 'under the hood' (in other words, your personal psychology) than what's in your wallet.

Having said that, life is such that we end up with the most powerful results when we apply a *combination* of mindset and strategy. That's why the entire Wealth Mechanic programme has been carefully fine-tuned so that each section clearly addresses either mindset (as you'll find here, in *Under The Hood*) or strategy (which is laid bare for you in the companion book entitled *Fix Your Finances*). Your journey toward a 100 per cent debt-free life is thus made simple to understand and easy to follow because of how it all unfolds:

- In this book, *Under The Hood*, we take a look at the so-called Big Picture, in other words the reasons you might be where you are today.

- Then we address why it's often so hard – despite your best intentions – to keep your hands in your pockets and your money in your wallet.

- Next, you'll gain a much clearer insight into who you are as a person, as well as the strategies you can use to turn *your* particular beliefs and values to best advantage.

- Finally, you'll master the simple psychology of the Galatea Effect in order to ensure optimum performance in your journey toward prosperity, freedom and abundance.

- If you then decide to follow on with *Fix Your Finances*, you'll be armed with the practical 'technology' of the Wealth Mechanic programme through a series of charts, worksheets, and examples that you can adapt to suit your own situation.

- Then you'll be able to select from a range of conventional and unconventional debt-bashing methods, techniques and strategies which you can rapidly put in place.

- Next, you'll ensure that your longer-term lifestyle dreams become reality as soon as possible. Best of all, I'll introduce a secret weapon that will help you forecast the exact month and year when you'll be financially free.

- Finally, you'll discover how to automate the debt elimination process so it takes place effortlessly – and so you can eventually concentrate 100 per cent of your efforts on building up substantial financial reserves.

You can also get the entire Wealth Mechanic programme between the covers of a single book. *Wealth Mechanic* combines all the material of *Under The Hood* and *Fix Your Finances* into a comprehensive 31-day step-by-step programme guide.

Buckle Up – From Now On, *You're* In The Driving Seat

Creating a sound financial future is a systematic process. Contrary to what you might start to think if you were to hire a financial advisor, the methodologies you use to create wealth in your life can be simple, straightforward and predictable.

Between the front and back covers of this book, you now have every tool you need to make a breakthrough change in your belief system, one that releases the grip of financial constraint so that *more money* can find its way to *you*.

What do you need to begin? Aside from a calculator, you already possess all the tools you need to fix your finances. If you don't believe me, stand up and take a good look in the mirror. *You're* the one who can fix this. You can take charge of things from now on. Believe it. So buckle up, and let's delve into the psychology that underpins the Wealth Mechanic programme.

Understanding The Credit Culture

Many people wake up one morning to find themselves overburdened by debt. Whether through loss of income, unexpected bills, or a sudden change in circumstances – life can suddenly feel unmanageable. More commonly, though, the build-up to a financial crisis arrives by stealth, which is what happened to me. I began at an early age to rely on credit cards to pay for the lifestyle I felt I deserved, hoping against hope that a bolt from the blue would eventually come along and save me.

Discover Why So Many Of Us Drive With The Needle On Empty

In hindsight it's no surprise that debt eventually turned my life into a living nightmare. But when did it all start to go so wrong? Though it took me many years to see it, my I-want-it-right-now attitude was at the core of my eventual debt downfall. Like so many people, I was simply spending money I didn't have.

As a teenager, I would have never guessed there'd be many 'tears before bedtime' in the years to come. On more than one occasion I ignored valuable lessons that were right in front of my nose, insights that could have helped me avoid the problems I eventually had face up to and pull myself out of. My first bout of overspending arrived on four wheels. With my sixteenth birthday less than a year away, I had my sights set on a new car.

But there was an unexpected hitch in my plans. I wasn't the first teenager in Southern California to be told, 'If you want a car of your own, that's great – only you'll have to get a part-time job and earn the money yourself.'

> **Though it took me many years to see it, my I-want-it-right-now attitude was at the core of my eventual debt downfall**

Fair enough. So I did just that. My first proper job was cleaning a chimney flue in a local steak house on Saturday mornings. I was very thin as a boy and was perfect for the job. More often than not I was covered from top to toe in brown sticky soot by lunchtime, but it was a perfect job for a kid who was on a fast-track plan to owning a set of wheels – market forces meant I was paid seven times the minimum wage. Soon enough, I had the keys to my very own car.

However, I had yet to learn that freedom has its price. I'd go to the filling station, top up the tank, and zip around town as if the thing ran on water. After six months or so of getting from A to B in my old banger, I became convinced that there was something seriously wrong with it – after all, this car was ten years old. I began to worry that there was a hole in the fuel tank. And that could be *dangerous*, couldn't it? A second-hand car was a bit like a pet dog; it required a lot of looking-after.

In my family, when there was something wrong with your car you got it on the blocks and fixed it yourself. I told my Dad about my concern, so he had a look under the hood. 'Well, the gauge seems fine to me. Put it up on the blocks, and let's have a look.' He slid underneath, and eventually remarked, 'I don't see anything leaking – have you been smelling fuel or something?' Of course I hadn't, not once. In hindsight, I'm sure he knew the real reason all along.

'No, it's just that I'm at the filling station every other day. It can't be right. I can't keep this up.'

My Dad, he's got a fairly dry sense of humour. 'I think I know what's wrong, Max,' he announced ominously. You'd better go in the kitchen and get your mother's calculator and a notepad.'

He wrote on the top of a sheet of notepaper I had fetched from the kitchen drawer:

MILES

Then he paused for dramatic effect,

PER

Another pause,

GALLON.

'So where do you go after school, Max?'

'Um. You know. Here and there.'

'How many *miles* do you do in a week?'

'Eh? No idea!'

'Well, let's say this heap gets 20 miles to the gallon. How many miles do you do in a day?' We lived in a rural farming community, so I took a guess at 30. 'If so, you're going through a gallon and a half of petrol a day. Right?'

What a rigamarole! I thought we were just going to fix the car. 'All I know is that when I fill 'er up it doesn't even get me through the week. And it's actually more than I can afford.'

He pretended to crunch out some numbers. 'Let's see… we have to live with the miles per gallon… We're stuck with the cost of fuel… What can we play with here? How much do you spend right now?'

It was more than ten dollars a week, but I wasn't about to admit to that, was I? I had things to do, people to meet and places to go. 'A bit over five bucks, I think.'

'Can you actually *afford* five dollars a week?'

'I guess not,' I answered, although I knew that my social life would be taking a serious hammering if I stuck to what I could afford.

'Theoretically, how much fun would you give up if you found some way of doing what you do on less than five bucks a week?' By this point I was spending a small fortune at the filling station. It was hardly what I'd call *fun*. It was annoying.

My Dad could probably see that my eyes were beginning to glaze over. After all, what good is a car if you don't *drive* it? What he didn't realise was that I was using a credit card, and had only been paying the minimum balance for the last few months. If this went on any longer, he'd be on to me. My only way out was to change the subject. 'So, there's nothing wrong with the fuel tank, then? I thought it had a leak.'

My Dad knew from experience that the Big Lessons in Life come up again and again if you ignore them the first time round. What I like about him is his patience; if you don't connect the dots he doesn't make a big to-do of it. In this particular case, I didn't get it and he didn't push it. I wish I had absorbed the lesson he was trying to make me understand at that young age. It might have saved me years of grief down the line. Indeed, freedom has its price.

CHAPTER 1

FASTEN YOUR SEATBELT
What we'll be covering this trip...

☞ Score your relationship to your finances with an 8-point personal evaluation

☞ Learn what it takes to begin to feel comfortable with your money

☞ Understand 'money' as a concept

☞ Realise how easy it is to forget that money has an intangible value too

☞ Form an accurate understanding of debt

"Man's mind, once stretched by a new idea, never regains its original dimension"

Oliver Wendell Holmes, Jr

I don't know about you, but I don't consider my personal finances a 'hobby'. It's a bit like washing the dishes or doing the dusting; it has to be done every so often or things get a bit out of hand. Having said that, unlike washing the dishes, failing to face up to your personal finances can affect every aspect of your life. Let's do an evaluation to try to figure out why you might be a bit short at the end of the odd week.

An 8-Point Evaluation of Your Finances

1. **When you stop and think about your personal finances, how does it make you feel?**

   a) Fairly self-assured

   b) A bit nervous

   c) Panic-stricken

2. Do you know how much your household spends each month?

a) Yes, I know exactly how much

b) More or less

c) I have no idea

3. If your present source of income suddenly stopped for a while, how many months could you stay above water?

a) At least nine months

b) Somewhere between three and nine months

c) Anything up to two months, if I'm lucky

4. How much of your overall income do you spend each month?

a) Less than 90 per cent

b) Somewhere between 90 per cent and all of it

c) More than what I actually have at my disposal

5. Do you regularly find yourself taking advantage of the overdraft facility on your bank account?

a) Once in a blue moon. I can't remember the last time

b) Sometimes things are a bit tight and I have to use it

c) I'm always in overdraft

6. Do you pay the full amount you owe on your credit cards each month?

a) Always

b) Sometimes I do, but sometimes I carry it forward

c) I only ever manage to pay the minimum amount

7. How much of your income actually goes toward the repayment of your debts?

a) Less than 10 per cent

b) Anywhere from 10 per cent to a third

c) More than a third of what I earn

8. Have you written down a financial plan or strategy for your household, and if so, do you look at it regularly?

a) Yes I do, and I adjust it from time to time

b) I sort of have an idea in my head

c) No. I don't have the time for boring things like that

For every answer you chose (**a**) give yourself three points.

For every (**b**) allow two points, and

For every (**c**) allow one point.

20-24 points:

Great stuff. You have the kind of mindset and strategy that will see you through to longer-term success with your finances.

For a more comprehensive test and an automatic score and assessment, go to our website: **www.wealthmechanic.com/assessment** *(using this VIP passcode to gain access: WM37).*

15-19 points:

You are aware of what you need to do, but perhaps you haven't yet put an action plan in place that utilises your finances to best effect.

0-14 points:

You would benefit from getting a stronger sense of your financial situation – and you'd do well not to wait a moment longer. You will profit greatly from a plan that takes you from where you are now to where you'd like to be in the future.

Sure, It's A 4-Letter Word – But It's Not *'Naughty'*

One in eleven people in Britain report being in debt or in arrears. A 2008 report by the mental health charity Mind reported that for some people, debt is 'a pathway to mental health problems.' In fact, Martin Lewis, author of Thrifty Ways for Modern Days, *proposed in October 2008's* Therapy Today *magazine that young people today are 'educated into debt' but not 'educated about debt,' adding that 'This is something we are not gong to be able to move away from as a society, so we need to be able to deal with it.'*

Most people are more willing to talk about their sex life than their finances. For some reason there's something unseemly about it. It's a topic best avoided. Yet debt is reaching epidemic proportions all across the country.

Something is obviously wrong if the average family is said to be spending 20 per cent more than it has coming in each month.

Insolvencies are approaching 300 casualties a day across the British Isles alone – which is far in excess of the records set in the early 1990s.

As such, about six million families nationwide are believed to be straining under the obligations of credit repayments. Citizens Advice Bureau expresses growing concern at seeing a million people come through their doors each year with debts that exceed their annual take-home pay.

Nowadays more than 60 UK households a day are so in debt that their energy supply is cut off. In fact, many families are at best a pay-day or two away from complete financial meltdown, and a staggering fifteen million of us are said to be plagued by almost continual thoughts of financial ruin.

Fact: Money Troubles Can Kill You Dead

Money troubles can take a toll on us emotionally, ruin our health, and put untold strain on our relationships:

Americans are responsible for more than $750 billion of debt in the form of credit card debt alone, according to a 27 November 2007 National Consumer Law Center report.

Mother of two Jane Parry returned home from work in July of 2004 to find her husband dead. Front-page stories reported at the time that Mr Parry had taken his own life at the age of 36. He had racked up debts of some £75,000 (that's around $150,000), an astounding £50,000 ($100,000) of it in interest and charges. On his modest salary of £25,000 ($50,000) he was juggling sixteen credit cards at the time of his tragic death.

A year later Robert Allen, a 53-year-old machinist, took his own life after amassing debts of nearly £100,000 (that's an eye-watering $200,000 worth of debts) – most of it on 23 credit cards he'd been juggling for years.

Mr Allen felt unable to keep up with the interest payments and penalty charges, so he wrote a note for his wife, Laura, asking her to deliver the bad news to his work colleagues and his team-mates at the Radcliffe Hospital Cricket Club – reminding her to check his lottery ticket on the Saturday night. Leaving a fiver to cover a bill for the newspapers, he finally asked for her forgiveness, and then hanged himself in their garage.

The ability to manage money grows with age and experience, but rapidly changing economic and social trends mean that today's 18- to 40-year-olds are faced with greater challenges,' according to John Tiner, chief executive of the Financial Services Authority in the 1 April 2006 Scotsman.

'They have greater access to credit and are becoming consumers at an earlier age. The cost of not having the necessary skills to make sound financial decisions is becoming increasingly significant.'

Mike Dawson, a 42-year-old self-employed consultant, chose an autumn day that same year to escape the pressure once and for all. He drank a bottle of whiskey, swallowed a handful of painkillers, and walked into the sea near the family's south coast home.

Leaving his wife Carol and their two teenage children behind, he had been in the process of remortgaging the property when the bank turned the screws, seeking eviction because of £4,892.66 (that's no more than $10,000) in mortgage arrears.

You might be saying to yourself, 'I wouldn't pack it in over a £5,000 debt.' But clearly, and tragically, a number of UK families in the past few years have paid the ultimate price.

An Unexpected Bolt From The Blue

Some people are hoping that a lucky break will save them, perhaps in the form of the next bonus cheque that will obliterate a four-figure overdraft, or the someday-one-day promise of inheriting Aunt Margaret's beachfront apartment.

A lot of us have mentally pencilled in a version of someday-one-day, but it doesn't always show up on the calendar as planned. If you don't take action in time, the problem *won't* go away. It will only get worse. This is what we all need to realise about debt. While you're biding your time and saying your prayers, the clock is ticking. Days turn into weeks; which turn into months; which turn into years.

Some of us can avoid taking control of our finances for a very long time. Many seem to be able to carry on driving with the needle on empty for quite a while, but that feeling of impending doom puts pressure on every day of our lives. In the back of our minds we all dread the day when everything comes to a grinding halt.

They Don't Teach This Stuff In School

So where did you learn what you know about money and finance? Most of us are never taught anything at all about the 'mechanics' of money, so it's not surprising that so many of us end up in a financial mess. Sure, we know how to write a cheque – some of us even balance our chequebooks. Whether we earn very little or tens of thousands a year, few of us were taught the fundamentals about:

The noted Harvard sociologist Daniel Bell proposed that capitalism depends on consistent hard graft, but also on peddling the ideals of hedonism and self-gratification. This keeps people spending, and eventually the whole idea of self-sacrifice goes out the window. And the 10 November 2008 issue of Fortune magazine noted that 'Millions joined in the debt mania,' proposing that, 'Today might be 'the ideal moment to make thrift cool again, because debt has rarely been in worse repute'.

- What to do with the money we earn

- How to plan our finances on a month-to-month basis

- How to invest for our longer-term future

- How to manage loans and credit

- How to plan for our years of retirement

Many of us just stumble and bumble our way through our finances – and hope for the best. But don't fool yourself into thinking this is all something to do with a person's so-called social standing.

Most would say that anyone taking home £60,000 a year was 'comfortably well off' (and $120,000 a year isn't bad, is it?). Yet the Consumer Credit Counselling Service says that those with incomes ranging from £40,000 to £60,000 ($80,000 to $120,000) still can't seem to control their spending. In fact, many people coming through their doors owe more than £100,000 (yes, $200,000) – and that's over and above their mortgages.

Without question, debt knows no class boundaries. Debt doesn't care whether you're a taxi driver or a neurosurgeon at a private hospital. It gets on top of a lot of us. Some people in debt are earning hundreds of thousands a year. Others are on state welfare benefits. What they have in common is that they are all spending more than they earn.

Every year people on UK state welfare benefits borrow £330 million from high-cost doorstep loan companies. Perhaps this is because some eight million low-income consumers cannot get mainstream credit.

According to an August 2005 report by the National Consumer Council, those who stick to cash are less likely to lose control of their finances or be in arrears.

Debt is debt, no matter how you slice it. You can be destroyed by it whether you owe $500 or $500,000. It's all relative, and you can journey down this road for many years without realising you've lost your way. Many people end their days as impoverished pensioners eating tinned sardines in tomato sauce because that's all they can afford. And that's not what our 'golden years' are supposed to be about.

More Than Just Your Personal Pile Of Poker Chips

Before we move on to the subject of what 'debt' actually is, we have to be honest with ourselves about the simple but often misunderstood concept of money.

What have we actually got hold of when someone hands us a nice big stack of banknotes? At first glance, money is just a symbol, a unit of exchange. When we're on the clock, we sell our employer our time for an agreed price, and no matter what we have in hand, it only goes so far – we have to live with what we get. Whether you exchange time, skill, objects or experiences, you seldom receive something without parting with something else.

But this is only part of what money means to us. Beyond the fact that it is a powerful unit of exchange, its power lies more often in the intangible value we place upon it.

Turns Out Aunt Mary's A *Loan Shark*

Okay, so what is *debt*? Why is it so taboo to say the word out loud? At its simplest, you are in debt when you've asked someone to lend you a tenner, although more commonly you owe an institution, such as a bank or loan company.

Anyone who is in debt knows that it's not just banks and building societies that end up giving us loans. We borrow from employers to get travel passes; from loan companies to pay for education; from business colleagues; from friends; and of course from kindly relatives.

In fact the most frequent kind of loan request goes something like this, 'Be a pal – can you sub me twenty until payday on Friday?' Or, 'Mum, Dad, we want to get a place of our own. Can you help us out a bit with the deposit?' You might call

According to the US Census Bureau's 2008 findings, US banks accrued some $643.5 million from credit card interest charges in 2006.

these 'soft' loans, in that a relative is usually not going to send the heavies around should you have trouble making payments.

In the next chapter, we're going to look in more detail at the different kinds of debt most people tend to encounter on a day-to-day basis. It isn't just another four-letter word.

THE NUTS AND BOLTS OF THIS SECTION

☞ In most households, money is a taboo subject

☞ Debt eventually gets on top of a lot of us, but it tends to happen without warning

☞ Ignoring the problem won't make it go away

☞ Money is just a unit of exchange

☞ It's not only the banks that give us loans. The most common form of debt happens between two people

CHAPTER 2

FASTEN YOUR SEATBELT
What we'll be covering this trip...

☞ Distinguish 'secured' from 'unsecured' debt

☞ Perform a One-Minute Debt Diagnosis on yourself

☞ Acknowledge the many get-into-debt influences that tempt us all

☞ Understand that lending is a business, and you shouldn't take any of it personally

☞ Believe that, no matter how complicated, every problem has a solution

> *"In the long run, we shape our lives, and we shape ourselves. The process never ends until we die. And the choices we make are ultimately our own responsibility"*
>
> **Eleanor Roosevelt**

Good faith alone doesn't always cut it in the big, bad world. Have you ever had a wallet, handbag, or bicycle stolen? It's not very nice, is it? When we 'secure' something, we are doing our best to make it safe. In fact car loans and mortgages work with this same principle in mind – you are generally expected to safeguard the financial stake of your lender or creditor (i.e. the company who risks the uncertainty involved in extending to you a line of credit).

A Gentleman's Handshake Means *Nothing* These Days

For all intents and purposes, when you secure a loan on your car or your home, you drive around or live in what's known as the 'collateral'. Life has its unexpected twists and turns, so you usually have to pledge something you own that is worth

Of those planning to buy a car, one person in four will finance the purchase with a loan, according to March 2006 figures compiled by the Sainsbury's Bank Car Buying Index.

more than the value of the loan. This collateral is put up as security; it's what makes the loan a safe bet.

People prefer to lend money under a secured arrangement because *you* are the one who takes the rap if you can't keep up the payments. In a worst-case scenario you'd be handing the lender the keys to your car or your home.

Many banks will raise interest rates for reasons other than delinquency, according to Consumer Action's 2008 survey or card companies. The so-called 'universal default provision' allows them to increase rates at any time based on consumers' usage of other lines of credit.

No matter who you are, you cannot protect a loan on the basis of your handshake, your word of honour, your signature, or even your spotless credit report. A handshake means nothing without collateral.

It's the same the world over: when we borrow money without *pledging* something of equal or greater value, it can prove to be our undoing. Credit cards, overdrafts and personal loans are some everyday examples of such 'unsecured' debt. This takes many different forms, and most of us encounter it on a day-to-day basis.

More than twenty million UK consumers spend nearly £5 billion a year on store cards. Yet the 21 March 2004 Independent on Sunday *reported that this accounts for just 2.5 per cent of total consumer debt. Credit card use is preferred by the vast majority; it's the payment method of choice for 60 per cent of Britain's consumer spending.*

Unsecured debt has a sting in its tail, because you have nothing in the wings to back it up – nothing to hand over to the loan company. Consequently, if you don't pay up you can get a bad credit rating, which could close

doors in your face for years to come. Moreover, it often costs more to borrow under an unsecured arrangement because higher interest rates reflect the lender's heightened risk.

Here's Your 60-Second Debt Diagnosis

1. You pay the 'minimum payment due' on your credit card each month, usually a token sum that does little to chip away at the actual balance.

2. You buy a wedding gift from a department store website, and charge it using your high-interest store card.

3. You unexpectedly need $500 to go to Malta for a funeral, so you get your overdraft extended by $750 until the end of next month.

4. You need to buy an annual travel pass for the year, and your employer advances you the money, then takes it out of your salary every month for the next twelve months.

5. You get one of those 'courtesy cheques' from a credit card provider, and you use it to sort out Christmas shopping – or maybe to tide you over so you can do justice to the January sales.

Courtesy cheques can be expensive. Payments made on these cheques are typically treated as if they were a cash withdrawal, so the debt incurred with them is charged at a higher rate of interest than would be the case on purchases made with the 'flexible friend'.

6. You buy a nice leather sofa on one of those interest-free credit deals where you don't have to pay anything until six months after it arrives.

7. You ask your employer for an advance on your next pay cheque and use it as a sort of 'bridging loan' to get you through until next payday.

Unsecured debt is:
- *Cash that you borrow without securing it with something of equal or greater value*
- *Credit that is extended to you*
- *A product or service you accept without paying for it at the same time*

How many different ways have *you* gone into debt using one of these methods in the past year? Or maybe something similar? Can you perhaps add seven more ways you've gone into debt? Welcome to the fraternity.

Asleep At The Wheel For Miles And Miles

Debt isn't an issue from day one, of course. It happens over time, by stealth. We don't even see it coming until it bites us in the back-side. Months or even years can go by before something knocks us out of our reverie. Our ability to remain in denial is akin to being asleep at the wheel for miles on end.

The financial services industry is said to have put a favourable spin on racking up debt. We don't even call it 'debt' anymore; we call it 'credit'.

Have you ever 'come to' at an intersection and thought to yourself, 'How the deuce did I end up here?' Maybe you missed a turn a few streets back while you were daydreaming, and had to turn around to head back the other way.

C'mon. Admit it, you've done it too – hopefully not in your car! We all do it at one time or another with nearly every aspect of our lives – and it's particularly easy to do it with money. Then one day we 'pull over', often in the midst of a financial crisis, and wonder where we are.

Keeping The Wheels On The Road Ain't So Simple

Have you ever 'accidentally' put the wrong cheque in the wrong envelope, a supposed 'mistake' that buys you more time to pay the bill? Or have you ever – how can I put it – 'forgotten' to sign the cheque? This is just the sort of juggling act *many* of us get up to at one time or another.

So, what's the deal with the three 'white knights in shining armour?'
Our nation's economy would grind to a halt without banks, credit cards and mortgages. It's just that some of us bite off rather more than we can chew.
Banks *make their money by lending us money. The thing is, they expect more back at the end of the deal than what we borrowed. This is what is commonly known as compound interest.*
Credit card companies *make their money by allowing us to spend a lot and repay very little. This is compound interest with a kick.*
Mortgage providers *make their money by helping us buy houses. They too expect to get back more than what was borrowed – that's why they sometimes end up owning the keys to our front doors.*

If you're really good at this kind of game, you can keep a lot of balls in the air without letting one drop. But whether you're rich or poor, whatever you are juggling has a habit of falling to the ground with a thud – eventually. In the meantime, does it help to know that the vast majority have firsthand knowledge of what it's like to struggle with today's credit culture, even if they hardly ever drop the ball?

Before you start to put into motion a sensible strategy for clearing your debts and building a better future, it helps to understand how easy it is to 'play games' within the credit culture – and it helps to see how *you* might have, however innocently, chosen to be a part of it. As a matter of fact, a lot of people who use credit play games with it – not only with plastic cards, but just as easily with

Whenever you use your UK credit card to pay for something that costs between £100 and £30,000, Section 75 of the Consumer Credit Act forces the card issuer to share liability with you if something goes wrong with the UK-based purchase.

In the US, the Federal Reserve Board outlines similar protection under the Fair Credit Billing Act, so long as the cardholder notifies the creditor within 60 days of the purchase in dispute, and pays any partial amount that is not in dispute.

household bills, family members, and friends. It all happens so quietly, and it all seems so harmless. But at the end of the day, the biggest games we play… we play with ourselves.

It's Easy To Lose More Than Your Shirt

That said, there are times when each and every one of us is caught with the legitimate need to borrow money. Whether it's to tide you over until your next payday or to finance the purchase of something big like a new car, just be careful – when you make the wrong choices it can cost you more than your shirt.

In principle, there's nothing wrong with taking out a loan – although it depends a lot on what you're borrowing it *for*. Some purchases warrant going out on a limb, but many in all likelihood do not. Don't get me wrong, a properly managed loan can, of course, be a useful tool.

It's just that there are temptations all around us, powerful influences that beckon us to spend more than we can often afford. And bowing to the pressure of those temptations is so *easy* nowadays. How many offers for loans and other forms of credit come your way in a week? Magazine inserts, newspaper adverts, junk mail, and television commercials – just for starters – literally bombard us each and every day with the chance to spend beyond our means.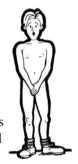

Nothing Just 'Happens' By Itself

Yes, it's fair to say that if you don't have a get-out-of-debt-and-stay-out plan, somebody will have a get-into-debt-and-stay-there plan to torment you with. Indeed, when it comes to money management, nothing just 'happens' by itself. There's always *some* sort of strategy or plan at work – either yours or somebody else's.

Credit isn't just a convenient way to pay for purchases when there's nothing in your wallet – it is a multi-million pound industry whose aim is to sell a smorgasbord of financial services to as many people as possible. And to do that, this industry constantly needs to perpetuate the illusion that being able to buy now and pay later gives the majority of us a greater sense of purpose, a happier lifestyle, and increased peace of mind.

Without a doubt, not many of us could write a cheque to buy a home for our families. And a lot of people would say that going into debt to put a roof over your head is the smartest investment most households could make. But then there's so much temptation to fill that home with lifestyle purchases that, generally speaking, are not smart money in the longer-term – particularly if they are bought 'on tick'. A lot of families get from A to B in a car bought on tick, sit on a sofa watching a widescreen TV bought on tick, sleep on beds bought on tick, and wash their clothes in a machine bought on tick. Before they book a sunny holiday with their credit card, they compare prices online with a buy-now-pay-later, state-of-the-art multimedia computer.

> With only a hint of irony, the 5 April 2005 Evening Standard put two headlines side by side: 'Feelgood Factor Fuels a New Craze for Cocktails' and 'Priory Clinic Blames Stress for the City's Drinking Habit'.
>
> In the article on the left-hand, a supermarket spokesman was quoted as saying, 'A cocktail boom is a good indicator of prosperity.' Sales of exotic gin in particular were up by a staggering 75 per cent from the year before.
>
> But in the article on the right-hand, Dr Neil Brener of the Priory cautioned, 'Almost 4,000,000 British workers are dependent on alcohol.' He argued that many people feel the need to 'self-medicate' in order to deal with their day-to-day problems.

Conspiracy Theory: All Part Of A Carefully-Crafted Plan

Credit was evidently first used in Assyria, Babylon and Egypt 3,000 years ago. Before banknotes, the 'bill of exchange' was common in the 14th Century, where debts were settled with one-third cash and two-thirds bills of exchange. Paper money didn't come into its own until the 17th Century. From the 18th Century, tallymen sold clothes in return for weekly payments, keeping a 'tally' of what was paid versus owed with notches carved onto a wooden rod.

So what actually happens when you buy something today and pay for it tomorrow? Well, the dozens of banks and lending companies out there have no choice but to *charge you* – in one form or another – for borrowing money that has their particular name on it. This alone is what gets a *lot* of households into serious trouble. But we all have to face up to the fact that lending is a business, so these companies are going to tear a little strip from each and every banknote you borrow. Thus the name of the game in the credit industry is to keep you in as much debt as you can manage, for as long as you can manage it.

Who knows? Maybe there *is* a conspiracy! Perhaps it's not an accident that so many people struggle for years with financial troubles hanging over their heads; perhaps it's all part of a carefully-crafted plan. And this is why you need to have a plan of your own, one that will *get* you out of debt, keep you out of debt, and put some money into your *own* coffers instead of the many 'credit-culture vultures' out there.

Believe me when I say that your situation is no better and no worse than a thousand other people out there. You wouldn't be the first person to tell yourself at this stage, 'The odds are stacked against me, and it would take a miracle to turn my situation around.' If this is the sort of talk kicking around between your ears, remind yourself that the credit-culture vultures placed a get-into-debt-and-stay-there plan right in front of your nose, and you fell for it – that is to say, *until now*.

From the moment this get-out-of-debt-and-stay-out plan begins to unfold, you will be armed with every tool you need to pull yourself out of a financial hole – and stay out. You've got to believe in what is possible. After all, problems always lead to solutions for those of us who choose to help ourselves.

THE NUTS AND BOLTS OF THIS SECTION

☞ Nobody can guarantee a loan on good faith alone

☞ When you borrow money without pledging something against it, the results can be catastrophic

☞ Debt happens over time, by stealth

☞ It's easy to 'play the game' within the credit culture

☞ There's actually nothing wrong with taking out a loan

CHAPTER 3

FASTEN YOUR SEATBELT
What we'll be covering this trip...

☞ Distinguish credit cards from debit cards

☞ Understand the concept of compound interest

☞ Realise that money means different things to different people

☞ Unearth childhood memories about money

☞ Believe that you can be in absolute control of your finances

> *"The farther backward you can look, the farther forward you are likely to see"*
>
> **Sir Winston Churchill**

Where I grew up, the Cold War was on people's minds, and we seemed to give a lot of thought to nuclear weapons, political brinkmanship, and the end of the world. People used to joke that one day President Reagan would get a bit nervy while shuffling papers in the Oval Office, and – in the manner of the best *Spitting Image* sketches – might accidentally rest his elbow on the fabled red button, bringing an end to the world as we knew it.

Cockroaches and Plastic Will Always Outlive You

Either that, or the same thing would happen on the opposite end of the world, and the missiles would head straight for the White House. This was more than a passing concern for me: midway through my time at university I was awarded a place in Washington DC, and I'd have been right in the

According to the National Consumer Law Center, for every home in the US there are twelve credit cards. And credit cards have become so popular in the United Kingdom that there are now more cards than people carrying them around, according to a March 2004 survey by the Office of Fair Trading.

firing line! One thing everybody in town knew to be true: the last survivors would be cockroaches and plastic – and my view at the time was that life without 'plastic fantastic' would not be worth living.

Long after the Cold War ended, debit cards entered the fray, providing a *Star Trek* version of writing a cheque – the effect on our bank accounts being identical, but more immediate. On the other hand, with a credit card, we are taking out a loan; we're buying on tick. There is no other way of looking at it.

Please be clear on the distinction between debit cards and credit cards. Know that debit cards are likely to be more and more commonplace, and try to think of them as 'Star Trek cheques'.

Now, I still have a chequebook, but I sort of have to dust it off when I use it. In addition to credit and debit cards, the world of today is one of electronic payments, online banks, web-based holding accounts, chip-and-pin, and cordless swipe terminals. And this trend will most certainly continue apace.

What exactly is 'compound interest' on a loan? Compound interest describes what happens when you're being charged interest on interest.

Suppose you borrowed $100 and the interest rate was 5 per cent per annum. At the end of the year you'd owe $105. At the end of another year, the compound interest would be 5 per cent of that $105, so you would owe £$110.25. At the end of a third year, the compound interest would be 5 per cent of that $110.25. And so on..

Are You Addicted To 'Plastic Crack'?

Do you notice how easy it is to just make the minimum payment on a credit card, month after month after month? And you know what? The banks that are handing them out willy-nilly actually don't mind if you *never* pay them off.

Like any other business, banks are in the game of making money. The longer you're hooked, the better. With many cards, if you were to consistently pay no more than the minimum monthly payment, you would end up shelling out nearly *four times* the cost of what you actually bought.

When I first started to apply the tools in the Wealth Mechanic programme, I did something drastic with my plastic: I went cold-turkey. I cut them all up. You see, I preferred a crisp wad of 'readies' in my wallet, so I could *see* them and *count* them. However, this isn't always a good move for a variety of reasons, as you'll see if you decide to read the companion book *Fix Your Finances* (where much is said about the debt-repayment flexibility that credit cards actually provide). So maybe for now it's more sensible to stash *your* stack in the back of a kitchen drawer.

Working with people who've followed this programme or attended my seminars, I've encountered some real creativity. Martin, a freelancer, gave all his credit cards to his mother-in-law, and had to ask her permission on anything he wanted to purchase. As you can imagine, it was very effective!

Many people have a variation on, quite literally, freezing their credit cards. (It's a great metaphor, as well). Sanjay and Mel, both 30, put theirs in a bag of water and stuck it in the freezer. Given that you could easily defrost it in the microwave, another couple closed this loophole by putting their cards in a baked bean tin, filling it with water, and then freezing the tin. (If you put that tin in the microwave, you'll have fireworks before you know it).

A 'minimum payment' is the lowest payment a given company will accept. If it's a fixed payment – such as what you pay toward a car loan or a personal loan – the monthly payments are set in stone. On a flexible payment – like the ones paid to credit card companies – the minimum amount they'll accept constantly changes in relation to your remaining debt.

I've known others to conceal their cards in a darkened corner of the attic, or even bury them in the back garden. It depends on how much your Dr Jekyll trusts the will of your Mr Hyde.

The Psychology Of Today's So-Called 'Credit' Culture

When you whip out your credit card, what you're doing is getting compound interest to work against you, not for you. Just remember, as old-fashioned as it is, most places still take money.

Money means different things to different people. It can be used to tell us something about love, approval, status, power, reward, self-worth, success, independence or freedom – to name just a few.

Money can do all *that*? No wonder so many of us tend to go through so much of it in a week. In the form of debt, however, money can cause us to experience self-punishment, fear of failure, rejection, dependency, self-recrimination or humiliation – and a whole lot of *other* unpleasant things as well.

Yes, it's easy to pave the way with the best intentions, and somehow end up on the road to rack and ruin instead. But why? To my mind, the credit culture is firmly linked to our childhood memories and our formative experiences with having a coin or two in our pockets.

Through a unique set of experiences, you began to see that money could conjure up feelings of pleasure (an afternoon at the skating rink, ice cream cones, or comic books) or lead to the sensation of pain (your parents having an argument, your cousin's hand-me-down clothes, or mum having to go to work), and you noted it down – probably unconsciously.

Let's Take A Drive Down Memory Lane

I would take a guess that your place in today's credit culture harks right back to the mental notes you made way-back-when. What do you think about credit – and about money itself – today? Do you love it? Do you hate it? Do you fear it? *Whatever* you think, it can probably be traced back to a set of long-forgotten experiences that you can count on the fingers of one hand. If you could access those distant memories, they might tell you a lot about how you see yourself and others around you. It helps to reflect on a set of questions, to step back in time, and to see the extent to which those formative financial experiences influenced who you were as a young person – and who you are, on some level, today.

Try as much as possible to re-live these experiences: where were you when such things happened? What else was going on around you? Were there other people around you? Were there arguments? Was there an underlying sense of resentment? Was there laughter, and if so, of what type? How did all this make you feel at the time? In other words, when asking yourself the questions below, try to place your memories in their proper context.

- Did you generally receive money as a birthday gift?

- If you received money for birthdays, was it followed by a bit of advice on what to do with it?

- Did particular relatives always give you a card with some money in it, instead of spending the time to purchase a gift?

- Were you given money every single time you went to see certain relatives in your family?

- Do you remember receiving particular gifts that you thought were extra special? If so, why *those* particular gifts?

- At a certain milestone in your life, were you given a weekly allowance? How was the 'spirit' of an allowance explained to you?

- Did you have to do any household chores to receive a weekly allowance, or was it just given to you outright?

- Did older brothers or sisters get a bigger allowance than you? Or did your next-door neighbour get a bigger allowance than you?

- Did you ever steal chocolate bars from the corner shop or steal pocket change from others in your house?

- Did your next-door neighbour have games and toys you didn't have?

- Did your friends at school typically have nicer or more style-conscious clothes than you did?

- Were you somehow ashamed to bring your friends to your family house?

- Did your friends at school book better family holidays than yours?

- Did the families of your friends have newer cars than the one your parents had?

- Did your mother need to work during the day while you were at school?

- Did your parents frequently argue about money troubles?

- As you got older, did you start to realise that either your mother or your father hid things they bought, in order to avoid an argument?

- In your teenage years, did you start to compare your family's lifestyle to that of your friends and neighbours, and somehow feel ashamed by what you drew from that comparison?

You may find that one particular memory, or cluster of memories, stands out in your mind. If so, you are gaining an insight into how you most likely relate to today's culture of easy credit. Once you have considered these thought-provoking questions, you will begin to see how vividly your first financial forays colour the way you think of credit, debt, and money itself.

What Does It Mean To Have Nothing In Your Wallet?

Isn't it interesting how much influence these memories can have on how we choose to interpret what's happening today? Even if we aren't 100 per cent conscious of those memories (and the vast majority of us are not), they are kicking around in our heads all the time – often determining our lifestyles far more than our education, our capabilities, or the amount of money we have in the bank.

It was certainly the case for me: when I look back at my first glimpse of adult life – a part-time job and my very own set of wheels – the interpretation I had begun to form about having a bit of money in my pocket seemed to heighten my sense of self-worth. So, naturally enough, when I didn't have any money I'd simply reach for my 'flexible friend'. Week after week I was pouring into my car's fuel tank what I wrongly mistook for freedom and independence.

No Matter *How* Much Trouble You Think You're In

In a nutshell, *Under The Hood* maps out the mindset for achieving *genuine* freedom and independence, and locking those sensations in place – permanently. Having said that, the resourceful changes you will master also launch you on a course that positively affects every other aspect of your life. And the good news is that it *doesn't matter* how deep a financial hole you may have dug for yourself – this book will be a valuable tool no matter what your circumstances.

Some people don't worry about money, and rarely give debt a moment's thought. Others have a growing sense that they're losing control, slowly but surely. And many feel completely overwhelmed by their debts.

Let's move right beyond those feelings of 'overwhelm' toward a proven methodology that can cut you free from your debt, help you stay free from it forever, and move you toward a lifestyle of *genuine* prosperity – all with the same money you're bringing in right now.

Not One For Penny Pinching – Are *You*?

I feel as if I ought to assure you that I'm not one for penny-pinching. I don't want to see you lower your standard of living – in fact, I'm all for the exact opposite. Just for the record, I would be pleased to see you dramatically *increase* your expectation of what life ought to be about, starting right this very minute.

This methodology isn't about eating tinned sardines and re-using tea bags, nor is it about working two jobs and surviving on five hours of sleep. What *Under The Hood* will do is lay the groundwork for getting shot of your debt once and for all – no matter how much you owe, or how long it took you to get to where you are today.

As we prepare to move on to the next section, try to set aside any hardened or cynical thoughts… Have faith: I'm not going to start telling you how you can make hundreds a week stuffing envelopes from home – this isn't one of those harebrained 'get rich quick' schemes. It isn't an investment strategy either. And I am not going to help you clear your debt by becoming bankrupt.

Lastly, I won't have you 'chanting for a Mercedes' or mindlessly repeating affirmations that you've stuck to your bathroom mirror. These breakthrough changes in belief system are the foundation of a 100% proven system *you'll* be able to use to climb out of your financial hole in a practical way.

The Wealth Mechanic programme really does work. It works in any city in the world. It works from any financial starting-point. For that matter, it works in any currency (I live in London, so my everyday currency is pounds sterling. London itself is a famously expensive city, and the examples given throughout the text reflect that). The principles are identical, no matter if your wallet is more likely to be full of dollars or euros. As a matter of fact, the concepts outlined herein are exactly the same the world over.

According to the 2008 annual US Census Bureau report, there were a total of 1,484,570 bankruptcies filed in 2006, only 485 of them voluntary.

And bankruptcies in England and Wales hit a record high during the first three months of 2005, according to figures released by the Department of Trade and Industry. The number of bankruptcies was nearly 25 per cent higher than the year before.

Commenting on the British figures to BBC News, Steve Treherne of accountancy firm KPMG observed that a 'black cloud of debt' hung over the UK.

Throughout the next couple of sections, you'll begin to understand what might be holding you back, both in terms of how you think and what you do. For you to start achieving powerful lifetime results, it doesn't need to get any more complicated than that.

Change Can Be Predictable, Painless And Fun

Men continue to be more likely to become bankrupt than women, and in the UK have average debts of nearly £50,000 ($100,000), according to a March 2006 Insolvency Service report. Men in their 30s and 40s account for the largest group overall, with men in general exceeding 60 per cent of bankruptcies overall.

Having said that, before we continue on our journey, I need you to take on one simple but *essential* concept: no matter what caused you to be in your current situation – be it divorce, job loss, illness, or (as in my particular case) simply spending beyond your means each month – from this moment you can always be in absolute control of your finances.

Is that just a whole lot of hippy-dippy California psychobabble? Not at all. You will be able to understand and – more importantly – *apply* this simple programme even if you're on state welfare benefits. You'll find out how to virtually guarantee your own success, and how to have *so much* success that your present income isn't even a consideration. As you are about to discover, when you actually take the Wealth Mechanic's 'mindset' to heart, the results you start to see are predictable, painless, and immediate.

THE NUTS AND BOLTS OF THIS SECTION

☞ Debit cards are simply another way of writing a cheque

☞ Credit cards are simply another way of taking out a loan

☞ Banks are in the game of making money, just like any other business

☞ Cutting up your credit cards in a fit of pique isn't always a good idea

☞ Money means different things to different people, and what we believe often goes back to childhood

Recognising Your Self-Defeating Behaviours

If I'd once managed to be such a dab hand at fixing my own car, why did I have so much trouble learning to fix my own finances? In the late 1980s, I moved from the USA to Britain and began my career as an architect. Our office was on Piccadilly. Even better, it was across the road from the Ritz. Mayfair: the best address in London. Indeed the first day at work – after five years of a student lifestyle – I felt as if I'd somehow *arrived*.

When Warning Lights Flash, Pull Over And Peek Under The Hood

But by lunch hour my enthusiasm and my wallet had both suffered a bit of a setback. Our office of 350 people was divided into smaller teams, and as I was a new arrival, it was decided that my team should go out to lunch.

Have you ever gone out with a large group of people who don't know each other very well? It can be a bit awkward. My arrival in London was truly on my uppers: I was completely broke. So I ordered soup, a side salad, and (in my then strong American accent) 'tap water'. There was nothing cheaper on the menu. My colleagues were rather more lavish: it was determined that the bill came to £25 each (seriously, $50 – and this was twenty years ago!) plus service... yes, *each*!

What?!

I'd only hours ago been introduced to these people. I hadn't even struggled through a whole day's work yet! I waited for a kind soul to say something to rescue me, but nobody did. Shamefaced, I waited a bit longer. An eternity went by. Then I reluctantly tossed my plastic on the top of the pile. Somebody broke the awkward silence: 'Right you are. Oh – Miss, it's £25 on each of the cards. Cheers.'

Still smarting from the experience, I made an important decision on the walk back to the office: I resolved both to consolidate my student loans and to buy some much-needed 'self-respect'.

> *I resolved both to consolidate my student loans and to buy some much-needed 'self-respect'*

Brandishing a reference letter from my boss, I was given a bank account and a four-figure overdraft within the first week. Today it's not so easy to walk out of the door with all that in hand, but at the time it was music to my ears. I convinced myself that I was on the crossroads of a dream come true.

A young man in my twenties, I finally had money to burn. And burn it I did. There were plenty of temptations on a daily basis: breakfasts, lunches, dinners, drinks with work colleagues, new clothes, trips to the music stores, gadgets and gizmos, as well as my lifelong weakness for a good book. Now even I could spend £25 a day on fripperies, without even trying very hard.

A bit of a babe in the woods, I hadn't quite figured out that – for one reason or another – most of my work colleagues were able to sustain a lifestyle I couldn't support. But was I going to let that stop me? Here I was in London's Magic Mile. Old Masters and old money. What other twenty-something former 'farm boy' had gone for a swim in the stunning rooftop pool at the Berkeley Hotel? Drinks at the Savoy? Fortnum & Mason's Full English Breakfasts at £14.00 a throw? Cigars at the Reform Club? This was the life, and I wanted a slice of it.

In my circumstances I was behaving recklessly, but I just kept doing it. On one occasion we all descended on a shop and each bought hundred dollar neckties. That was far and away in excess of my grocery bill for the entire *week*.

Between paydays I would sometimes concede defeat, and keep my hands in my pockets. But on 'Lucky Fridays' my pay cheque would be burning a hole in my wallet. When I'd make my way

A young man in my twenties, I finally had money to burn. And burn it I did

past Tower Records, a little voice inside my head would say, 'There's nothing wrong with having a quick look around.' After all, I could save money by taking the Number 3 bus home. Top deck. Front seat. But I rarely went home empty-handed.

On the way I'd sometimes stop at the Piccadilly Arcade to pick up some shaving gear… at twice the going rate. 'Thank heaven they take cards,' I'd mutter, 'but I'd better buy a few more bits to make it worth it.'

For most of us, the more we earn the more we spend. We live for today. There's always 'too much month and not enough pay cheque'. In my case, there was a lot more to it. Every time I opened my wallet, it seemed to affirm that I was indeed part of the Mayfair smart set. My card was rarely declined, because in my head I kept score – and hovered just below the surface of my bank overdraft and my card limit.

By behaving as though I'd indeed 'arrived', I was able to fool myself and my friends for a surprisingly long time. When I walk around Piccadilly these days, my old stomping ground seems like a different world from the one I thought I understood so well.

CHAPTER 4

FASTEN YOUR SEATBELT
What we'll be covering this trip...

☞ Recognise your most self-defeating behaviours

☞ Accept the challenge of peeking under the hood

☞ Realise the positive aspects of making mistakes, and learn how to use them to best effect

☞ Initiate dramatic change through three simple questions

☞ Understand what you give up when you fail to create goals

> *"In any moment of decision the best thing you can do is the right thing, the next best thing is the wrong thing, and the worst thing you can do is nothing"*
>
> **Theodore Roosevelt**

Even the most finely-crafted Rolls Royce needs periodic maintenance. If you find yourself too distracted to pay attention to the odd squeaks and rattles, they can easily turn into problems that loom large. Regular attention to the warning signs is necessary to maintain the smooth running of any vehicle – and the same holds true for your finances.

More often than not, there are one or two 'warning lights' flashing for anyone on the journey toward problem debt. But it's no surprise that a lot of us tend to ignore them, either unconsciously or deliberately.

What would things look like if, at the next crossroad, you were abruptly forced to pull over, look under the hood, and assess your spending behaviour? Would you want to keep carrying on as you are? Do you have any particular problems with debts that feel as if they're starting to get out of hand? If so, what are some of *your* flashing lights?

The 16 'Warning Lights' You Ignore At Your Peril

Let's take a look at what might turn out to be one or two self-defeating behaviours you have found it hard to be honest about. Do any of these patterns of behaviour seem familiar?

Your Credit Cards:

1. Do you usually end up paying just the minimum amount due on your credit cards?

2. Have you ever paid off one credit card with a 'cash advance' using another card, just to take the heat off?

3. Are you hovering so close to the credit limit on one or more cards that you cringe as you hand them over the counter?

4. If you get an offer in the post for a 'pre-approved' credit card with a favourable interest rate, do you fill it out and eagerly run it down to the Post Office?

Your Car and Your Home:

1. Do you make hefty monthly payments on a car in order to 'look the part'?

2. When you finally do pay off your car, do you immediately trade it in for a new one?

3. Do you have a mental tab on how much you can go into debt, based on the current paper value of your home?

4. Have you ever remortgaged your home solely because doing so enabled you to clear some longstanding debts?

Your Other Debt Demons:

1. Do you usually get by from one pay cheque to the next without setting aside something for saving or investing?

2. Have you ever accepted a store card because the cashier enquired, 'Would you like to save 10 per cent on your purchase today?'

3. Have you ever had your telephone or electricity cut off because you didn't pay the bill on time?

4. Have you ever used a personal loan to clear a credit card balance, then taken the card back to its limit, thus forcing you to make payments on both?

Worrying about money troubles kept more than a third of surveyed couples awake at night, according to a report published by the Financial Services Authority in 2006. Money woes beat career problems and health scares as the primary cause of night-time restlessness.

Your Emotional Costs:

1. Do you lie awake at night obsessing about money problems?

2. When you finally face paying your bills or opening your bank statements, does it make your stomach churn?

3. Have you found yourself looking out for a part-time job in order to help clear off some of your debts?

4. Do you lie to your partner about how much money you owe, or do you hide your shopping in the wardrobe when you get home so no one knows how much you've spent?

A guilty one in five women hide their shopping from their partners and/or lie about how much they spend on clothing accessories, according to a July 2005 survey released by Churchill Home Insurance.

If you identify with a few of these self-defeating behaviours, you may regularly beat yourself up about it –

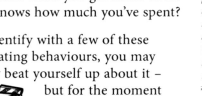

but for the moment let's leave the issue of blame at the side of the road, shall we?

Time To Take A Look Under The Hood

Nothing changes until *you* do – but when you do, *everything* changes. Why ignore the warning lights any longer? Let's pull over, put the handbrake on, and take a look under the hood. The moment you start facing up to your behaviours, you begin moving away from life's limitations, and toward the possibilities.

Peeking under the hood can be a big challenge though: nobody wants to get their hands greasy and look at this stuff. Some of us try to justify our behaviour; others just keep driving on – stuck in a state of denial about why things are in such a terrible state. The thing is, your behaviour always has a habit of catching up with you.

Let's Leave 'Blame' At The Side Of The Road

Sometimes getting it wrong in life is the best way to learn. Do you get the best mileage you can out of *your* mistakes? They're your most valuable commodity. We can learn, grow, and even profit from our bad-debt stories. Mistakes are often how we most effectively show ourselves the things we need to work on.

Karen McCall, founder of the California-based Financial Recovery Institute, proposed in October 2008's issue of Therapy Today *that we can explore our whole value system and sense of guilt and shame in life through the relationship we have with money.*

Though it's not always easy, try to see your errors of judgement as learning opportunities and nothing more. I'll repeat myself: let's leave the blame at the side of the road.

If you decided to believe that you were 100 per cent in charge of your own behaviour – being the one holding the steering wheel – then you would have to adopt the mindset that *you're* the one making things unpleasant. But it's sometimes difficult to adopt such a line of thinking. This might help: what if the only thing you could guarantee to change in this world was the person you see staring back at you when you look in the mirror? To genuinely live life through that belief – well, it's difficult to imagine how powerful that might be, and indeed what might be possible.

When we fail to take responsibility for our actions, on some level we've let go of the steering wheel and climbed into the back seat. But taking responsibility isn't about accepting the blame for a situation; it's got nothing to do with that. Taking responsibility simply allows us to step outside of the shame we have wrongly linked to past events, whilst letting go of nothing more than the fears and doubts we might be holding about the future. Having said that, keep in mind that there's a world of difference between knowing what we ought to be doing and actually facing the fears and doubts – actually setting out to *do* it.

We Can All Learn From Our Bad-Debt Stories

Many people know exactly what their repetitive mistakes are, and they know exactly what it would take to put a stop to them. But they fail to make the decision to *apply* that knowledge, and they just keep trundling along. For tens of thousands of people, it's as simple as that. Until they understand what they are doing on a conscious level, they repeat the same mistakes. So they struggle on, surprised when they suffer another setback. Once they begin to make a 180 degree shift in their decisions, they move forward more rapidly than they ever thought was possible, and in more areas of their lives than they expected.

So how do *you* begin to get the most out of your most valuable commodity for a change? We'll get to that, soon enough. But first you might need to face up to a thing or two. As you may have begun to realise, the Wealth Mechanic programme is about much more than fixing your finances – it's about fixing the whole of your life. It follows that there's a lot to be gained from looking at how you have lived your life up to now – and how you'd like to live it as the future unfolds before you.

Genuine Change Takes Shape From The Inside Out

Money worries are a significant cause of anxiety and stress for more than ten million Britons, according to leading mental health expert Dr Roger Henderson. In a 20 January 2006 report conducted on behalf of AXA, he found that one in every four adults cites money worries as having an adverse effect on personal relationships.

Fully half of those surveyed have more arguments when they are worried about money, one out of five complained of a sex-life slump, and more than a third spend less quality time with their partners or perform poorly at work.

Believe it or not, money really can worry us sick.

In order to bring about dramatic changes to how you are living your life, sometimes you have to ask yourself some very uncomfortable questions – and you have to look deep inside yourself for the honest answers. Indeed, genuine change starts from the inside and works its way out. There's no other way to achieve it. So here's the first question you need to ask yourself:

• Have I actually made the *decision* to bring about some positive changes to how I've been living my life?

Most people, when I ask them that question, say, 'Yes!' without blinking an eye. But many of them, at this early stage in the programme, haven't actually decided to change; that is to say, not *yet*. And there is a fundamental reason for this, something that holds true for each and every one of us: we never ever decide on something without first having a reason to do it.

When you make a decision to bring about a different set of outcomes – and you know your reasons for the decision – you have the essential ingredient for bringing about long-lasting change: desire. So the next question you need to ask yourself is this:

• What are my *reasons* for making the decision to change how I've been living my life?

It helps to know what makes you tick as a person. Some people avoid painful feelings, as in, 'I don't want to ever face another Final Notice from a utility company again.' Others gravitate toward upbeat sensations, as in, 'I want to have the money to be able to spend every weekend doing little day-trips, buying antiques and sampling village life.'

What Are *Your* Reasons For Wanting To Change?

Deep down, you probably have a dozen or more reasons for wanting to change. Once you have settled on a few reasons for deciding to adjust a thing or two, the next question you need to ask yourself is this:

• What are the three most resourceful changes I could make over the next 90 days?

If you were able to arrive at three specific changes that, once realised, would give you a true sense of accomplishment, then you are invoking what is known as a 'compelling future'. Compelling futures give you a taste of what is potentially on the horizon, and they kick-start you into doing whatever it takes to bring what's in the distance closer to home. But if you found it difficult to create a compelling future, you are not alone.

My observation is that many people have a tough time answering questions about their immediate or longer-term futures. Some people live for today, and don't want to step out of the here-and-now. Others are stuck in the past, forever influenced by the pain of the there-and-then. But if you can learn to do it – if you can learn to fix your eye firmly on the horizon – you will find it much easier to embrace growth and change. And here's the best news of all: this is something any one of us can practice and learn. And when you have mastered it to some degree, you will find yourself forever able to shape your own vision of the future. Eventually it becomes the predominant focus in your mind's eye.

Once You Know The 'Why', The 'How' Is Easy

Once you have developed a three-dimensional image of the view ahead, you don't necessarily have to labour over setting short-term and longer-term goals. You will find that your mind just sets them into motion. And every time you manage to achieve a positive change, your preparedness for growth and adventure is enhanced a hundred-fold.

But suppose you are still struggling with the questions posed on pages 52 and 53. Let us try to get in touch with a stronger sense of desire – indeed, if you know the 'why', then the 'how' often falls into place quite naturally. A word of warning… this next question might well be the most cringeworthy one of the bunch – particularly if you are finding it difficult to create a compelling future:

- If I could perform a *miracle* in the next 90 days, what are the three biggest changes I would make to the way I'm living my life?

Now, I'd like to invite you to re-word those three biggest changes so they present themselves as powerful statements of intent, like this:

- Within 90 days, I will wipe out the whole of my overdraft through reining in my daily spending.

By stating your desired outcome in this particular way, and by giving it a specific timeframe, you will create a *goal* to aim for. Never underestimate what you're giving up if you fail to create goals. A person without a goal is no more focused than a Sunday driver without a map.

Understand that a 'goal' remains no more than a 'dream' until it is given focus, shape… and a deadline. But there is more than this one set of distinctions between dreams and goals. Dreams characterise something we might well and truly long for, but there is no essential ingredient that makes us committed to the idea that they ought to come true. Here is a nice pipe dream: 'Someday, I'll win the lottery, and all my financial troubles will melt away.' But carefully-crafted *goals* should be both ambitious and attainable at the same time: 'Before my 40th birthday, I will leave my job and use my savings to open a seaside café.'

Never Knock A Person's Dreams – Especially Your Own

Keep this in mind when you are constructing a set of goals: you can't give shape to a goal unless it firstly arises from within a dream. Just make sure that *your* particular goals are congruent with your most vivid and technicoloured dreams. Only *then* can you measure your potential and mark your progress along the way.

But once you have gone through the trouble of framing a powerful set of goals on paper, don't just stash them away in the back of the kitchen drawer… Display them on the fridge door, so you can refer to them a number of times a day. These are statements of intent, not just something you are 'hoping for'. And when nobody is looking, read them aloud with absolute conviction, so you grow accustomed to how it sounds to hear yourself saying them.

Doing whatever it takes to move toward a new set of behaviours will slowly start to feel right. In the next chapter, we are going to take a look at some of the self-defeating behaviours that might be present in your life, habits that might have become so familiar over time that you are now *unconscious* to the price you pay for continuing to abide them.

THE NUTS AND BOLTS OF THIS SECTION

☞ The moment you start facing up to your behaviours, you begin the process of positive change

☞ Your past mistakes are valuable experiences. Getting it wrong is the best way to learn

☞ Taking responsibility for something has nothing to do with accepting the blame for it

☞ Genuine change starts from the inside, and works its way out

☞ Desire is the key ingredient for making lasting changes

CHAPTER 5

FASTEN YOUR SEATBELT
What we'll be covering this trip...

☞ Discover how easy it is to dig your head in the sand

☞ Recognise when a repayment strategy is flawed from the outset

☞ Beware of times when money seems no more than a bunch of numbers

☞ Accept that it is nobody's fault if you get 'passed a hot potato'

☞ Understand that 'interpretation' can either be your best friend or your worst enemy

"The thing we all call 'failure' is not the falling down, but the staying down"
Mary Pickford

A car's warning lights indicate faults or possible problems with the machinery. Some indicators are more serious than others, and we eventually find out exactly *how* serious when we ignore them for long enough.

Everyone knows the feeling of 'running on empty' when the needle has been in the red zone for the past few miles. Ignore it for too long and you'll be thumbing it to the next filling station. Yet in our personal lives few of us notice our most unhelpful habits and behaviours, because they have simply become automatic over time.

Let's see if you can gain some valuable insights from taking an objective look at another person's behaviour, before ultimately considering your own. You might make connections between these stories and some of the unconscious habits that could indicate self-defeating patterns in *your* life too.

The 11 Surefire Signs That You're Running On Empty

We all have our life strategies and little tricks – it's just that some of them actually make for a very stressful life. Let's see if you've ever caught yourself doing something similar to one or more of these warning-light habits:

1. The Cheque's In The Mail

'The cheque's in the mail,' Brian assures the woman who rings up from the credit card company as he's watching the evening news with his wife. That was a close shave. Inside, he's quaking in his boots and steps outside for a secret cigarette because he hasn't *really* posted the cheque. He and his wife have been arguing about their ever-increasing overdraft and the fact that they have racked up all their credit cards to the hilt.

2. Writer's Cramp

Kevin habitually opens his post, looks at the amounts due, and sticks the bills in the back of his desk drawer, so he can temporarily fool himself into thinking he's actually got money in the bank. He hates the fact that they all want 'his' money on a monthly basis. And he *really* hates seeing the word 'overdraft' on his bank statements.

'A debt spiralling out of control can often lead to relationship breakdowns or illness,' reports Ian Richards of the Insolvency Helpline. In fact, nearly one in five who lose control of their finances end up ill as a result, according to research he cites from a June 2002 study.

At the extremes, the situation can even foreshadow a heart attack. Moreover, people in debt apparently tend to smoke more, drink more, and are more likely to lose their jobs.

Kevin seethes every time he has to pay for something boring like last month's heating or telephone bills. He frequently complains that if there were *just one month* when all these bills didn't come at once, his bank balance would be looking good for a change. Because he's getting so far behind, Kevin is finding that he is getting more and more confused about what he actually owes.

3. The Archaeological Dig

Margaret doesn't even open her post. Her husband used to pay the bills, but since the divorce she tosses all the post into a *ginormous* bowl by the front door. It is a simple matter of procrastination. Once in a blue moon, when the kids are out, she steels herself with a glass of red wine, and dumps the contents of the bowl onto the dining room table.

She divides everything into four piles. First, she opens anything with a handwritten envelope. Things being well, it might be a birthday card from a relative – with a cheque. Then she opens the subscription magazines, and whatever else is safe territory.

She counts to ten, and begins opening the dozens of official-looking envelopes. The stacks of this unopened post create a sort of timeline, like thousand-year-old sedimentary layers. She first uncovers final notices ('*That* can't be right!') relating to reminders that arrived weeks beforehand. After some digging she finds the original fossilised bills at the bottom of the pile.

She realizes that before they cut off the electricity she should drop everything and give them a call. This is not a good way to spend a Saturday afternoon.

4. The Squeaky Wheel Gets The Oil

Stephan and Jean pay all their bills, but not always on time. They often put into place a strategy of putting off one or two bills until next month in order to stay within their overdraft limit.

All's well and good until 'Patches,' their son Billy's cat, has to go to the vet because she has cystitis – it's hard to believe that they charge so much for a drip feed, anaesthetic, an overnight stay, test results, and two follow-ups.

The problem is that they are so close to the line that this week they'll have to pay for the groceries with a credit card to bridge the gap.

5. The Bouncy Castle

George's view on life is that everyone bounces a cheque now and then, don't they? Or a few? George thinks he has a kind of 'sixth sense' about his bank balance. 'I can pay *half* of this bill, but will probably pay *all* of that one.'

One out of five American banking customers reported switching banks because of fees they considered to be excessive, while only one out of every 25 switched banks because of security concerns, according to an August 2007 survey of some 5,000 people conducted by Gartner, Inc..

The fact is that George never really understood money unless he could see it in his wallet. With banknotes and coins you can touch it, see it and feel it – but with one of those slips of paper spat out of an ATM machine, it's just a bunch of numbers.

When he goes to the cash point to check his balance, he gets a rough idea of where he stands, give or take…plus or minus, except for any cheques that haven't cleared.

6. The Waiting Game

Adam is proud to say that has never gone into the red in his life. A self-employed accountant in his late thirties, he *always* has a healthy bank account. He even balances his chequebook every month!

He has figured out a system to get interest-free credit, and plans every expensive purchase to coincide with the end of his credit card company's billing cycle. This gives him over a month and a half before he has to pay the balance. Hey, presto! It's pure magic.

Adam and his wife, Jane, decide to spoil themselves and go on a £3,800 holiday to Tuscany. He makes sure he purchases the tickets according to his 'system'. He forgets, however, that this system only works if nothing goes wrong.

Unfortunately, out of nowhere, Adam's two best clients file for bankruptcy within a month of his return. This surprise has put him completely on the back foot, with very little income and no payment-protection insurance – and yet the bills just keep coming in.

Approximately half the businesses that go bankrupt do so because they failed to safeguard themselves against the actions of customers who don't pay their bills, according to the Association of British Insurers in July 2005. Chris Hannant of ABI observed, 'Bad debts are bringing businesses to their knees.'

7. Ships That Pass In The Night

Suzanne and Warren are like a lot of households today: Suzanne works full-time in the City, and Warren is a freelancer who works from home. These two have a whole strategy for paying bills; they pay everything by cheque.

Here's what credit cards usually do: they make everything you buy cost a bit more than the asking price. When you buy something on credit, you pay interest over and above what you would with cash.

Barely keeping their heads above water, they make sure they carefully synchronize bill payments. For example, Suzanne makes sure she shops late on a Friday night, knowing the store can't process her cheque until Monday at the earliest. And then they'll have a few more days before the cheque actually clears. Bill payments and pay

That's why the guy next door who's paying cash for everything can, in reality, have a better lifestyle than you.

cheques cross in the post like ships in the night. With such delicate timing, it doesn't take much for something to go wrong; it's only a matter of time.

8. Fool's Gold

Kelly, a recent business school graduate, has a really good job. She is a very safe bet on paper – maybe that's why she seems to get Platinum Card offers every other week.

Kelly is forever transferring her growing debt from one 'precious metal' to the other, in order to take advantage of six months' interest-free credit – all the time vowing to cut up one of the tired old Gold Cards once and for all.

But where did she put the scissors? Slowly but surely, both the old cards and the new ones are all jacked up to the limit once again.

9. The Free Spirit

An inability to manage credit was given as the reason for the bad-debt stories of nearly half the respondents of a 2005 study by the Centre for Insolvency Law and Policy at Kingston University. Business failure, divorce, illness and redundancy were the next most frequently-given reasons.

Steve is a second-year student at Bristol University. He's footloose and fancy-free because there's more to life than looking after the pennies. Steve goes out every night, places his card behind the bar, and has no idea of what he spends.

After all, he figures that a couple of years from now he'll be in some boring job, married, with 2.4 kids in tow. He might as well live it up while he's still got the chance.

At the end of the month the bills come, and he always pays the minimum balance. It will come right in the end; it always does. Meanwhile, Steve gets on with the fun.

10.Cut Your Coat According To Your Cloth

Andrew was a foreman at a manufacturing plant until he was abruptly made redundant. He had never saved much of his middle management salary. It's been six long months, and the state welfare benefits don't go far. Yet he is still living the life he'd led before his circumstances abruptly changed. By continuing to spend as though he has a job, he is failing to adjust to the new realities.

The average wedding now costs £15,795 and the average divorce £25,575. Nonetheless, more than 160,000 UK couples tend to divorce each year, according to research cited in the 6 January 2006 Telegraph. Sean Gardner, chief executive of MoneyExpert.com, summarised, 'Divorce is on the increase, and Britain has one of the highest rates in the world.'

It's often terribly difficult adjusting to a sudden change in circumstances. It's not much fun, either. Being out of work is depressing enough, but having it foisted upon you without notice is doubly difficult. If only he had been given some kind of warning by his employer... The thing is, the situation is getting more urgent by the day. Andrew's inability to face the fact that things have taken a turn for the worse – however temporary this may be – means he is failing to cut his coat according to his cloth. And in those circumstances, it wouldn't take much to lose his shirt.

11.Pass The Hot Potato

Jim and Bridget have been married for seven years and have two children. Jim is still reeling over Bridget's recent news: she is seeing someone else, and wants a divorce.

He was married once before, and hardly gets to see his teenage son, despite child-maintenance payments that are eating him alive. And now he can expect more of the same.

'I didn't ask for this,' Jim fumes, 'so why should I be the one who's losing out?' He has been passed the proverbial hot potato, and his hands are *burning*. So he throws it in the air: without really thinking about the consequences, Jim abruptly stops paying child maintenance across the board. In the back of his mind he knows it will catch up with him eventually, but not right away.

Imagine: There's A Good Side To *Every* Bad Behaviour

Do any of these scenarios sound familiar? They are more common than you ever could imagine. In the next chapter, we shall begin to explore *why* we do what do, even when a habit does us harm. It's important to remember that we never do anything without a reason; these self-defeating behaviours all have pay-offs.

And it is extremely important to remember that sometimes events lie outside our control. We *can*, however, determine how we react to any of life's events; that's our power base. So, was Jim's divorce 'the end of the world' or was it 'the shaky start of a new beginning?' Like everything in life, however you choose to look at a situation, it's really nothing more than an interpretation – a 'story' you've made up so you know where to file it in your head.

Forty per cent of 18- to 25-year-olds use credit cards for their everyday living expenses, with one out of ten revealing that credit card payments are set against more than half their earnings each and every month.

As with the average bottle of white wine, it doesn't seem to improve with age: two out of five 26- to 40-year-olds would not survive more than a month if they lost their jobs, according to May 2005 research by MyEquifax.

Is the story *you've* invented about memorable events in your life somehow holding you back?

Maybe like Jim, you're divorced, and not only have you started a new household, but you have to pay a staggering amount of child support. Perhaps you didn't go to university; or possibly you've just finished, and your student loan payments have just kicked in.

Perhaps you're on state welfare benefits. Maybe you weren't taught anything about money. Perhaps your kids have had it a bit rough since your break-up, and this isn't so easy.

Maybe someone in your family has an unseen disability, or your own health situation is a bit unpredictable. Possibly you've been overlooked on a promotion you really deserved.

Sometimes it feels as if you're winning; sometimes it doesn't. There is really no point in trying to keep score. It's not a contest – and stop looking over your shoulder: nobody's keeping score on *you* either.

THE NUTS AND BOLTS OF THIS SECTION

☞ Your most unhelpful behaviours have simply become automatic over time

☞ We all do little 'tricks' with our finances, and many of them make for a stressful existence

☞ You never do anything without a reason; even your most self-defeating behaviours have a pay-off

☞ The only real control any one of us has is the ability to decide how to react to life's events

☞ The way you react to what happens in life is an interpretation; it's just a story made up in your head

CHAPTER 6

FASTEN YOUR SEATBELT
What we'll be covering this trip...

☞ Understand why New Year's Resolutions often fail

☞ Define what you are really buying when you go on a spending spree

☞ Recognise when perfectly normal activities head for a downward spiral

☞ Decipher the influences of fear, doubt and shame

☞ Know when you are in a state of self-hypnosis

"All the money in the world is spent on feeling good"

Ry Cooder

What do most of us do on New Year's Eve, besides drink cheap champagne as the clock strikes midnight? We make New Year's resolutions, don't we? The start of a new year always seems to be the opportunity for a fresh start.

We usually resolve to change a habit that we can't seem to shake: 'I'll stop watching so much television... I'll stop eating so many microwave meals... I'll stop gambling on the Internet... I'll stop staying late at the office,' and so on.

One reason that most resolutions fail is because we haven't examined the pay-offs we receive by maintaining these behaviours. Many of us who struggle with our finances fall into a series of habits that seem to give us

Barely 1 per cent of the British population struggled with a severe gambling problem in year 2000, according to the July 2005 issue of Therapy Today. *Citing the only nationwide study of the problem, it was found to affect some 500,000 people.*

On the other hand, technology can change things in a matter of years: over three-quarters of the UK's 29 million adult Internet users reported that they regularly placed a bet either online or offline, found Forrester Research in a 2005 report, according to BBC News.

the same sort of 'rush' as behaviours we would normally label as 'addictive.'

As a psychotherapist, I have encountered a whole spectrum of ways to define the term 'addiction': an inability to participate in the real world, some form of moral weakness, a lacking in willpower, a spiritual crisis – and even a *disease* of some sort.

Having said all that, most of us tend to think of addiction as the kind of 'misuse' that – in one form or another – does its thing by passing our lips. But maybe the whole issue isn't as simple as that.

Every Farm Boy Worth His Salt Knows This

No doubt about it: there are certainly so-called gamblers, workaholics and overspenders who eventually find themselves suffering the same sense of despair we more readily associate with substance misuse.

The feeling certainly sounds similar to what I myself felt when I was hopelessly overspending. On a day-to-day basis, I suppose I was invariably trying in vain to bring into my life three sensations that everyone in the world seeks:

- Purpose and meaning

- *Genuine* happiness

- Peace of mind

Having our fair share of each of these sensations isn't a lot to ask for, is it? Naturally there are times when we have one or more of them in our life to a greater or lesser degree, but we want all of them equally – and most of us want them full-on,

24/7. The reality is that none of us gets an equal share of these feelings at any one moment – but (as is the case with a three-legged stool) uneven legs can still provide a stable platform.

In hindsight, my own problem with overspending seems to have been an attempt to manage those moments when one aspect or another of this 'three-legged stool' seemed to break away. If I didn't feel equally supported by all three sensations at the very same time, things felt a bit wobbly underfoot.

How does a credit card make you feel? When you're given a credit card, you're not really given anything more than a thin piece of plastic that conveniently fits in your wallet. But you'd think these things were actual wafers of real gold or genuine platinum the way we revere them.

It's the feeling that somehow you've arrived; you're somebody important when that wafer of 'gold' or 'platinum' is stuffed through your letterbox. Believe me, it's just a piece of plastic.

Many of us fail to realise that when one of these 'legs' falls short for a while, without a doubt the others will still manage to balance and support us. But if we cannot accept that each of life's supportive sensations is actually meant to step in and out of our lives, we find ourselves at odds with the way the world is set up. We then search for other forms of contentment in an attempt to sustain a permanently upbeat mood.

I myself started to believe that the best way to 'take a happy pill' was through my silly spending habits. And you could say that I embraced life's highs. Who *doesn't*, in some form or another? But when the highs were absent, I wrongly interpreted what was happening as some sort of drug-like 'comedown'. Ultimately, though, the same holds true for all of us: it's all smoke and mirrors; just an *illusion* that we are filling some kind of emotional void.

What's In All Those Shopping Bags?

And yet somehow I believed that 'retail therapy' gave my life a sense of purpose and meaning, made me feel happy, and eased my mind. Thus the self-confessed 'shopaholics' aren't actually in search of clothes or shoes – though it certainly looks that way when an army of bags marches into the downstairs hall. Such people are simply trying to re-create an upbeat sensation, and who can blame them for that?

When under the *illusion* that shopping brings some form of emotional satisfaction, such people are actually trying in vain to fill their bags with something money can't actually buy. What sort of upbeat feeling might a person be attempting to buy, for instance, on a weekend visit to the shoe store? How about:

- A sense of power

- A sense of 'the good life'

- A sense of security

- A sense of abundance

- A sense of generosity

- A sense of importance

- A sense of 'being part of it'

- A sense of superiority

- A sense of stability

Hey, We're No Different From Cats And Dogs

So how do we know when we're possibly heading down the path of the problem spender? One day our connection with an everyday object or experience gives us the sort of 'rush' I mentioned at the beginning of this chapter.

The object might be a lottery ticket, the keys to a sportier car, or whatever. The experience might be a shopping spree, a lavish meal out, or something like that. You feel good, so you want to do it again. We all tend to move away from painful feelings and toward pleasurable ones: a bored lunch-hour window-shopper eventually discovers he can experience a brief shot in the arm through bagging a bargain at a seasonal sale.

So how do you put 'pleasure' into words? Sigmund Freud, the founding father of psychoanalysis, proposed that pleasure is quite simply what we feel when some kind of tension is relieved. That makes it sound as if we're no different from cats and dogs, doesn't it?

I'm a bit of a gadget man. And apparently I'm not the only one out there; it seems we all have the urge to splurge. A report entitled 'Shop Tarts' suggests that my obsessive search for the next new gizmo is something of a British national pastime.

Psychologist Dr Aric Sigman, who compiled the report, determined that the UK's voracious appetite for choice and innovation was statistically double that of shoppers in countries like France or Spain, according to the 6 February 2005 Observer

If that's all Freud had to say about pleasure, how do you suppose we humans manage to tidy it up in a box and put it in our shopping bags? We *can't*, that's the thing. Freud certainly got *that* part right!

Yet you might be wondering if there is actually any real *harm* in the average case of retail therapy. My personal view is that for many it's just a bit of harmless fun – but for others it can lead to the same self-damaging path as substance misuse.

Picked To The Bones By The Shopping Piranhas

The trouble is that at some stage otherwise perfectly normal activities start heading in a downward spiral. The internal conversation of a problem spender might sound something like this:

- 'I'm not exactly thrilled with my tatty old shoes, and I'd really like to hit the winter sales at lunchtime.'

- 'But I'm dead broke until pay-day. If I wait, though, everything will be picked to the bones by the shopping piranhas.'

- 'I'm so glad I decided to have a look, because there are all these great bargains; two for one!'

- 'I'd better call it quits here and now, because I've got to pay the rent on Friday… Wait a minute, I missed this: a matching belt. It would be madness to pass it by.'

- 'After all, it's worth the money if it makes me look the part at the office on Monday. That's what credit cards are for.'

The above internal conversation makes a person inclined to believe that a 'half-price bargain' is a dose of summer sunshine. When your underlying aim is to experience a spot of the old pleasure-in-a-box, your internal barometer is constantly gauging the weather, based on how much of it you seem to be getting.

Every Coin In Your Pocket Has A Flip-Side

When we make contact with these short-lived highs – consciously or otherwise – we often want to experience more of them. This sense of exhilaration is certainly an effective cure for boredom, but it's a high-stakes game to play.

If our behaviour develops into a longstanding habit, we inevitably become more strongly attached to the rush-like sensation, which can be very addictive.

Once we fall into this trap, and things are out of control, there is a flip-side to the coin: we can begin to feel debilitating levels of fear, doubt and shame. It might help to have a look at each of these struggles individually.

'The range of obsessions and compulsions that may become addictions in our society is growing. Indeed, the major conditioning factor in our society could arguably be said to be consumerism,' asserts Richard Bryant-Jeffries, *author of* Counselling for Problem Gambling, *in the March 2006 issue of* Therapy Today.

Consumerism aside, 'Gambling is the hidden addiction,' continues Adrian Scarfe of Gamcare. 'Mostly the Department of Health defines addiction as substance addiction, so other addictions like gambling [and] shopping… don't get the same recognition.'

The Truth Of What Money Can And Can't Buy

If we find ourselves 'chasing the rush', and the rush is that of spending (often with nothing in the wallet), then it's fairly natural that we start to become afraid of the eventual consequences. However, by that stage we're even *more* afraid of giving up the fun stuff. After all, what would replace the upbeat sensation?

This is all about what we focus on: how do *you* decide what makes you feel good? There is a lot at stake here. Take for example the sensations of *success* and *importance*: to feel successful or important, the problem spender is pinning his hopes on something that has a price-tag stuck to it.

Even more fear is on the horizon once it dawns on us that everyday objects and experiences lose their shine over time – and that there are a lot of things in life that money can't buy.

From clothes and shoes to gadgets and furniture, Britons spend more than £5 billion a year on the quiet, without their partners knowing. A January 2006 report by Egg Financial Services indicates that some £350 ($700) a year is spent on the sly.

Secrets And Lies... Secrets And Lies

Doubt sets in when we begin suspecting that we aren't always in control of our habits and behaviours. We don't want to acknowledge that we might actually be lacking in restraint. We begin to become plagued by all sorts of doubts – and then we begin to rationalise our behaviour in order to silence what we don't want to hear inside our heads. This is certainly a betrayal of ourselves, but we might also find ourselves increasingly betraying others:

• We start to blame situations or other people, even when we know this isn't part of the problem.

• We begin to tell little white lies to hide our behaviour or otherwise 'save face'.

• We start to withdraw from people we care about because it all starts to feel so awkward.

• We start hiding from our families some of the stuff we've bought, so we don't have to spring it on them all at once.

• The secrets mount up when we find ourselves intercepting the post or opening up separate bank accounts.

If you have ever caught yourself doing any of these things, you know how badly you'd like to make sense of your actions. Maybe, though, you can't. Instead you drown out your doubts with a few more denials and rationalisations in order to get a little bit of peace of mind.

Round And Round In A Vicious Circle

Because none of this self-defeating behaviour actually squares with who we believe we are, an uneasy sense of Sigmund Freud's 'tension' arises and we begin to feel shame. The problem with shame is that it has a tendency to perpetuate the behaviour: shame wrongly places the blame for a situation on 'who we are' instead of what we've done wrong.

If we make the mistake of believing that our spending errors characterise who we are as a person, we feel bad about ourselves – so we have the urge to spend once again in order to feel better about ourselves. We thus create a vicious circle: the more we try to find emotional satisfaction through problem spending, the more we encourage the green shoots of shame.

Although we sometimes carry a degree of remorse or guilt about what we've done wrong, it's a big leap to say that there is anything flawed about *who we are*. Shame has a lot to answer for, because we can't make amends if we believe that our errors of judgement arise from the core of our identity.

The antidote to shame is integrity, and the most effective way to reclaim our integrity is to take full responsibility for our actions. In doing so, we win back both our self-esteem and the esteem of others.

After all, let's be realistic: who do you know that hasn't made huge mistakes at some point while trying to get their emotional needs met? Just about everybody, right? Then it's important not to judge yourself in such an unforgiving light.

What To Do If You've Driven Down A Blind Alley

We are all *meant* to have emotional needs. We're also meant to fumble and bumble as we attempt to fulfil them. It's just that some of us eventually run down a blind alley, chasing after emotional satisfaction by grabbing hold of something that has a *price-tag* stuck to it.

Through problem spending we can sustain an almost permanent state of self-hypnosis – the illusion that we've achieved a sense of well-being and a retreat from the awareness of not being in control. This holds the false promise of a place where fear, doubt and shame can be temporarily absent. But to *stay* in such a place, we'd have to be asleep at the wheel on an almost continual basis.

There is a healthier option: meeting our emotional needs through relationships with ourselves, with our friends, and with the communities we belong to. These are some of the many things that money can never buy. But before we begin to make healthier choices, we need to start forming more empowering beliefs. In the next few chapters, we will undertake to look at this process in detail.

THE NUTS AND BOLTS OF THIS SECTION

☞ Many fail to make lasting changes because they don't understand the pay-offs they're receiving

☞ Everybody seeks to achieve upbeat sensations, but sometimes we do it in ways that later prove unhelpful

☞ Few of us accept that upbeat sensations are meant to blow in and blow out, just like the weather

☞ Much of your behaviour is an attempt to re-create a sensation you've experienced in the past

☞ When your behaviour develops into a habit, your attachment to upbeat feelings can seem 'addictive'

Identifying Your Self-Limiting Beliefs

Throughout the 'retail therapy' phase of my life, I couldn't yet see that I had fallen into the same trap as a lot of other people – a lifestyle based on credit cards made it easy to ignore how much I was spending each month.

Before Setting Off Again, Have A Look In The Rear-View Mirror

Behind my reckless behaviour, I'd been clinging to the belief that on landing a decent job, I would be on my way to untold success and riches: I'd finally be somebody who had 'arrived'. Until then – if I'm honest – I suppose I perceived myself as somewhat of a nobody.

Because I was a young professional with expensive tastes, I relied on overtime to make up for what my salary lacked. For that reason, I should have been a bit more worried when my boss pulled me aside one day for a chat.

'Max, can you come in here for a moment?' Being a bit old-school, Oliver always used the speakerphone – even though my desk was just outside his office. 'Shut the door. Please, have a seat.' Oliver was a good source of office gossip, so I pricked up my ears when he announced, 'There's going to be a meeting this Friday. All of us, top down. Both buildings.' He added conspiratorially, 'They're providing beer.' Alarm bells started faintly sounding off in my head. Free beer… I knew what that meant: bad news.

It became clear that I actually owed more than I made in a year

Sure enough, when Friday rolled around (to make matters worse, it wasn't even payday), we were told there would be no more overtime pay. We'd have to sign revised contracts. Times were tough, we were told. So, no more team pizzas on expenses if you worked late. No more personal phone calls unless you paid for them… The list of restrictions droned on.

'This can't be happening,' I thought. 'My life is over.' I felt like jumping off London Bridge with weights around my ankles. You see, by then I'd gotten myself into quite a spot of trouble. I was still spending money I didn't have – often juggling credit cards to get me from pay cheque to pay cheque when my overdraft was up to the limit. And without any overtime pay, my number was finally up.

I had no real sense of the figures at the time, but it later became clear that I actually owed more than I made in a year.

Desperate times called for desperate measures. With my tail between my legs I decided I'd have to ring up Grandpa Jack in California.

He was always an early riser. 'GOOOOD MOOOORNING,' he roared down the phone; sharp as ever for a man the wrong side of 90. If you waited to ring much later than 6 am, he'd be glued to the set watching the New York Stock Exchange on cable TV.

Who likes asking a relative for a loan? There's something a bit shaming about having your back that far up against the wall. By then I had branded myself a failure, and I finally had to admit I needed help.

'I suppose you're not ringing me up all the way from London to talk about the weather, are you?' I told him about my plight. 'Sounds like you've got yourself in quite a pickle, Max.' Without skipping a beat he then asked, 'D'you know how to play poker? How many suits are in your average winner's hand?'

Bewildered, I mumbled that my troubles were well beyond a lucky break at a game of cards. But it wasn't just a bad attempt on his part to make light of the situation. He told me that the four suits in a financial winner's hand were:

• Investments

• Business ventures

• Education

• Good ol' bricks and mortar

'Not every venture in life pays off,' he said, 'but this is how a really smart guy stacks up his poker chips.' Oh boy. Here was Grandpa Jack with another Big Lesson in Life. But I continued to listen as he took me on a walk down memory lane. He reminded me that when I was a child, my parents had moved our savings accounts to a local community bank. It was then that Grandpa Jack gave us kids our first taste of investing.

You've got to learn to tell good debt from bad debt

He'd bought each of us a handful of shares, and remarked at the time, 'If we're going to give them our money, we might just as well have a piece of their bank.' Eventually later this bank was bought out by a branded chain, and everybody concerned did rather nicely.

Neither he nor I would soon forget the time when, aged eighteen, I tried my hand at what seemed to be a promising business venture. Grandpa Jack had stumped up start-up capital of $1,000. That was a small fortune to me at the time; all the more so when it soon went down the drain.

'Congratulations! Your very first business failure,' he'd consoled. 'It's good to get it out of the way while you're still young. *Most* people fail the first time round, and probably even the second – but it's only a failure if you didn't learn anything. Tell me what I got for my money.' The more we'd talked about what had gone wrong, the more I realised there was a lot to learn about the big bad world out there.

No surprises that after my entrepreneurial disaster I'd decided to go to university instead. If I brought the receipts for my academic books, Grandpa Jack often paid for the purchase. 'You're a smart kid. Put as much time and money as you can into your education.'

Grandpa Jack was quite switched-on when it came to property, as well. 'But to win big at bricks and mortar takes a different kind of smarts.' He always said that real estate was really a numbers game – and a game a lot of people *lost* unless they really knew their stuff.

Suddenly, he brought the conversation back to the present day when he cautioned, 'Max, you've got to learn to tell good debt from bad debt.' Then he announced his decision regarding my loan request: 'The way I see it, I like to play the four suits when it comes to opening my wallet. However, for a lot of the rest of life, it's important to keep your hands in your pockets... Here's the deal: for the same reasons you learned to fix your own car, you're going to have to learn to fix your own finances.' This wasn't the answer I was aiming for, but it was very clearly the answer I got.

CHAPTER 7

FASTEN YOUR SEATBELT
What we'll be covering this trip...

☞ Recognise the ways in which you spend small sums each day

☞ Accept that we *all* harbour conflicting beliefs about ourselves

☞ Understand that cultural imprints affect you unconsciously

☞ Discover the missing ingredient when your attempts to change turn out to be short-lived

☞ Identify the three rules of thumb for adopting empowering beliefs

> *"Our lives improve only when we take chances,*
> *but the first and most difficult risk we can take*
> *is to be honest with ourselves"*
>
> **Walter Anderson**

It's plain to see that I had fallen into the same trap as so many people: a false identity based on credit cards made it easy to forget how much I was spending each month. But who did I learn this from? It just didn't add up. My parents have always been sensible – they certainly wouldn't choose to have breakfast at Fortnum & Mason every other day.

When I had a good look at myself, I realised that, really and truly, my debt dilemma had nothing to do with the sudden lack of overtime at the office. Behind all the bluster and bluff, I came to see how stressful it had all become, trying in vain to keep up with the spending habits of the people around me.

Credit card company providers are becoming understandably concerned over increased losses. According to a March 2008 article in Business Week, *US card providers reported some $38 billion in bad loans from the year before. Columbia Law School researcher Ronal Mann reported that rate reductions would not be prone to affect repayment patterns.*

The total outstanding credit market debt in 2006 reached $12.8 trillion (more than £6 trillion), according to the 2008 US Census Bureau report, and the total liabilities due to consumer credit alone reached $2.4 trillion (more than a trillion pounds). '

It may be the same for you. When we spend everything in our pockets each month (or even worse, spend a little bit more), we steer ourselves down a road familiar to many – a journey beset by a whole spectrum of 'what-ifs.' What if I can't keep all the balls in the air? What if I'm 'found out' as a fraud? What if this reaches the stage where my back is finally up against the wall?

And the biggest 'what-if'of all? What if I don't have enough money when I retire? Yes, I'll get a free bus pass and reduced admission to the cinema, but will I be able to survive on a state retirement pension? I may be facing a life of tinned sardines, re-using teabags, and staying at home every night watching TV.

Who's Actually Picking Your Pockets?

A 2004 survey by British Insurance found that four out of five British homeowners regarded meeting their mortgage payments as the biggest financial worry if they were to lose their jobs.

What about you? Your pockets are probably a little bit deeper than they were ten years ago. But have you got any more money saved? Lots of us think of the equity in our homes as money in the bank, but aside from that, what else is in the kitty?

Suppose things went a bit pear-shaped for you? It has been said that many of us are only two or three pay cheques away from being out on the street.

I'm going to hazard a guess that you aren't as silly as I was, running around Mayfair having thirty dollar breakfasts to give myself a taste of the high life. I'm sure you think I was being a bit ridiculous, and I'm not going to argue with you. But don't miss the point here: don't get hung up on the fact that my weakness was posh nosh in the Big Smoke. It could have been *anything.* You'll have *your* way of picking your own pockets – and those little habits can go unnoticed for a very long time.

A lot of financial troubles have nothing to do with how much goes *into* your pocket each month; it's what gets taken *out* that causes the problems. This holds true whether you receive state welfare benefits each week, or make that same amount of money in an hour. The more we earn the more we spend – it's as simple as that for most of us. That is certainly what got *me* into hot water, and it's also undoubtedly why many of us have so little money put away for a rainy day.

The last few chapters provided you with an opportunity to get in touch with some of your self-defeating behaviours. In this section, we are going to explore the nature of what, generally speaking, can make people drawn toward behaving in ways that are harmful and counter-productive. We will also try to pinpoint the specific manner in which you might well be sabotaging your own best intentions – without even realising it.

Eighty-three per cent of those who became insolvent did so quite simply because they had spent more than they earned. Research conducted by Pricewaterhouse-Coopers in 2005 thus challenged conventional wisdom that life events such as job losses are the main cause of insolvency.

The Galatea Effect: Confused And Conflicted

I hold the view that there is a common thread running through the core of each and every one of us: our *identity* determines our behaviour patterns every step of the way – and our identity takes shape as a result of our *beliefs* and *values*, which influence pretty much everything we do.

When I eventually took a hard look at my own identity, I discovered some things that surprised me – *especially* when it came to the subject of money. On one level, I believed that 'having money' was the first step toward achieving my every desire in life, and that nothing would really fall into place without having rather a lot of it.

Through my eyes, so many things appeared to be terribly constrained by lack – and such an impression had inevitably coloured both the value I placed on money and what I believed it could bring into my life. In fact, money was part of an enormous 'salad bowl' of confused and often conflicting beliefs and values about self-worth and my very identity – especially in relation to how I saw myself alongside other people. This 'mixed salad' formed a belief system that I had swallowed wholesale without digesting the constituent ingredients.

I have no doubt that the same will hold true for you. In fact, we *all* have funny ideas about money that arise from our families, our friends, our backgrounds and our communities. In most cases, none of these beliefs and cultural values is spoken about explicitly. Although little is said out loud, they somehow echo and reverberate for years.

Until you are in the situation yourself, it is difficult to imagine the damage credit card debt can do to both your net worth and your self-worth.

From the list below, make a mental note of which statements ring true for you, and at the same time consider how many other statements could be added to the list from *your* internalised voice:

- 'Money commands a certain amount of respect, no matter who you are.'

- 'There's no such thing as having too *much* money.'

- 'Money can't buy you love.'

- 'The whole idea of being in business is to charge as much money as you can get away with.'

- 'People with very little money lead miserable lives.'

- 'Too much money just burns a hole in your pockets.'

- 'Money alone can never make a person happy.'

- 'Big dreams don't come true without the money to back them up.'

- 'It takes money to make money.'

- 'Some people are just too lazy to go out there and earn proper money.'

- 'Money makes the world go around.'

- 'You need to be ruthless in order to make tons of money.'

- 'All the good ideas for making money have already been thought of.'

- 'It's better to give money than to receive it.'

- 'Some people have so much money that it's actually *offensive.*'

- 'Ordinary people have to work hard for their money.'

- 'It's just not right to charge money for certain things.'

- 'Getting hold of money is all about *who* you know, not *what* you know.'

Some of our most deep-seated beliefs and values ignite the desire to experience sensations such as power, security, stability, importance and success. Interestingly enough, these particular qualities are strongly identified with the struggle many people have with what is or isn't in their wallet. In the previous chapter you explored some of the ways in which *you* might have been behaving in an attempt to experience these sensations. Now you are being invited to consider the more fundamental issue: whether your unique perspective on these sensations is unconsciously working *against* you.

And Where Did You Get *That* Idea From?

Keep in mind that most of us tend to hang on to a lifetime of unhelpful beliefs we've gathered along the way. And if we are not careful, they can prove to be treacherous – especially the beliefs we hold about *ourselves*. Here's why: some of life's biggest struggles seem to come about through a mismatch between our actions and the set of beliefs and values we unthinkingly store in our heads.

Cultural imprints in particular appear to leave stubborn and indelible marks on our identity – but there's every reason to take heart. Asking the right sort of question expands and evolves any person's frame of reference. This is about questioning the very essence of your current relationship with money. Only then can you begin to relate to the money in your pocket in a fresh new way.

In cadence with the passing of the US Congress's $700 billion bank stimulus, on 30 September 2008 the number on the US Debt Clock showed $10,150,603,734,720, exceeding the capacity of the digital readout.

Once you peer through the haze of your own limited thinking, it helps to ask a series of probing questions: from where did I get these beliefs? Is it helpful to hold on to them? Has holding on to them caused me to behave in a habitual manner? What identity would I be forced to let go of, were I prepared to redefine these particular beliefs?

Ultimately, what you are able to get in touch with through asking such questions is a current measure of your own 'self-belief'. Whether you like it or not, your relationship with money is sensitive to the folklore of your past – but it is also elastic. Each new experience has an effect on whether you continue to fear money, resent it or squander it… or whether you begin to handle it with confidence and ease.

The Worst Kind Of Brainwashing We Do To Ourselves

Below are two of the most elementary facets of self-belief. Consider the shape of your current identity as you take a good look at these aspects of yourself in the rear-view mirror:

• Your beliefs about what you are capable of achieving in life

• Your beliefs about who you really are as a person

The ways we choose to frame the beliefs about *who we really are* tend to colour every aspect of our lives. That's why we need to change our way of thinking before we can make lasting changes to our behaviour. But it's much more of a challenge to redefine 'who you are' than it is to change a behaviour. Let's look at the difference between these two bits of 'internal conversation':

• **I've been acting recklessly with my credit cards.'** (A sensible expression of remorse about what you've been doing wrong in a particular aspect of your life).

• **I'm a reckless person.'** (An unhelpful expression of *shame* about how you define yourself as a person).

The scary thing is that once you choose words to define 'who you are', your behaviour will tend to be consistent with the definition you've chosen. Labels you've created for yourself can be bad enough, but how about the labels you've been given by others:

- **'He's a reckless person.'** (A label that you'd tend to internalise if you valued or respected the person who said it when referring to you).

With unhelpful beliefs still kicking around in the back of your mind, one thing starts to become apparent: when you try to change your behaviour, your successes tend to be short-lived. The reason? You are fighting against the internalised definition of 'who you are' the entire time.

For example, as part of my *own* exploration of the mindset that underpins the Wealth Mechanic programme, I realised I needed to confront a label I'd been given as a teenager: 'Of all the kids, *he's* the one who can't seem to handle money.' Inside my head I immediately stored the message, 'Of all the kids, *I'm* the one who can't seem to handle money.'

Powerful Change Has Nothing To Do With Ability

After taking a look at myself, it was hard to accept that somewhere along the way I hadn't redefined that bit of identity acquired all those years ago – but I realised there was little mileage in blaming anyone else for saying it. I had to focus instead on bridging the gap between the identity I'd continued to wear and the identity I wanted to try out for size. Believe me, it was less about changing what I was capable of, and more about how I continued to define myself.

This holds true for all of us: changing our behaviour is generally not enough, because over the long haul, we tend to behave in a way that's consistent with our definition of who we are – even when that identity is self-limiting.

You see, the great majority of us are not the least bit conscious of our 'stories' about ourselves; and when this folklore is unconscious, it tends to be what's pulling the puppet strings – it tends to control how we think, how we behave, and how we respond to the world around us. We define who we are in countless ways. Here are some of the more everyday examples:

- **By your role:** 'I'm a single-parent.'

- **By your job:** 'I'm a schoolteacher.'

- **By your education:** 'I'm a Cambridge graduate.'

- **By your past:** 'I grew up on the wrong side of the tracks.'

- **By your future:** 'I'm on the way up in this company.'

- **By what you're not:** 'I never venture south of the river.'

To really begin to define who you are, it is first essential to distinguish your limiting beliefs from your more empowering ones. After a while, limited thinking tends to stand out – and it tends to do so from a mile away. If you have the slightest inkling that one or more of your beliefs is stopping you in your tracks, it helps to ask yourself, 'Is this really *who I am* or simply *how I've acted*? Well then, who shall I decide to be, from this day onward?' That, in the words of the Bard, is indeed the question.

Here's How To Jump-Start *Your* Success, Right Now

When you wish upon a star, the little things you quietly mutter on a moonlit night should not be taken lightly. Empowering beliefs tend to be sculpted from your roughly-hewn wishes and desires. Having said that, keep something in mind: spoken words fade to a whisper over time; what shouts loudest is said with pen and ink. That being the case, it is most effective to use a notebook when crafting a more empowering set of beliefs. How about rewriting a chapter or two of your own book of folklore?

In a moment, I am going to invite you to begin to replace some of your limited beliefs with ones that are far more empowering. But before you become acquainted with this potent technique, here are a few rules of thumb that should be taken into account:

1. **Always phrase your empowering beliefs in the present tense, like this:**

*   I am in total control of my finances.

*   I possess sound judgement every time I purchase something.

*   I am well on the way to personal wealth and success.

2. **Always ensure that your empowering beliefs are short, snappy and easy to commit to memory, like this:**

*   I am 100 per cent free of debt.

*   I am a dab hand at managing my personal finances.

*   I have more than enough resources to meet my needs.

3. **Always go out of your way to avoid placing constraints on empowering beliefs, like this:**

*   I am *within* three years of leaving my nine-to-five job.

*   I am depositing *at least* $25,000 a month into my business account.

*   I am setting aside *no less than* 10 per cent of my income each and every month.

Before this chapter concludes, I invite you to use your notebook to have a go at transforming your most all-encompassing 'limited belief' into what might end up being your most empowering one. Just remember this: when your beliefs are shrouded in fear, they won't fall by the wayside without a fight.

You need to puff up your most empowering beliefs so they are larger than life itself – and *that* simply means they need to be much brighter and more vivid than worries about your car payment, anxieties about your credit card bill, and the persistent strain of a four-figure overdraft. Have fun with it!

THE NUTS AND BOLTS OF THIS SECTION

☞ Your identity takes shape as a result of your beliefs and values, and this determines how you behave

☞ Some of your biggest struggles arise from a mismatch between your *actions* and your beliefs and values

☞ The ways you choose to frame the beliefs about 'who you really are' colour every aspect of your life

☞ It is more of a challenge to redefine who you are than it is to change a behaviour

☞ When your 'folklore' is unconscious, it tends to control how you think, behave and respond to the world

CHAPTER 8

FASTEN YOUR SEATBELT
What we'll be covering this trip...

☞ Recognise when you are telling yourself 'little white lies'

☞ Understand the 'chain reaction' between thinking, behaviour, and results

☞ Evaluate five common problem-spender identities

☞ Discover your top three fear-based beliefs in relation to your finances

☞ Connect the dots between beliefs and emotions

"Don't ever let your beliefs limit your horizons"
Brian Smith

What might be keeping *you* from conducting your life in a way that leads you steadily toward financial freedom? For many people, it is simply a matter of one or more limiting beliefs that stop them in their tracks. In order to reach a state of financial well-being, you first have to believe you can *do* it – and then your behaviours need to contribute to that belief, not detract from it.

Is the folklore you've invented about your life holding you back? Within the mindset of the Wealth Mechanic programme, we begin to take an honest look at our most unhelpful beliefs about who we think we *are* in life. Haven't you ever caught yourself drumming up a little fairy-tale about yourself? Little white lies such as, 'I don't really care if I never have money.' Or 'Wealth would only give me a big headache and extra responsibilities.'

Perhaps you have accepted the folklore that someone *else* gave you about who you are. Stories like, 'You're a terrible fool when you've got a bit of money.' Or maybe they cut you right to the quick with, 'You're one of those people who'll never amount to anything.'

No matter what sort of mess you might be in at this point in time, there is nothing wrong with wanting to have more out of life than you have right now. So don't for a moment feel hesitant about raising your standards and broadening your expectations. On the other hand, if you continue holding on to the belief that it is impossible for you to have more, you'll be 'tapping on the brake pedal' throughout the remainder of the explorations in *Under The Hood*.

Do You Harbour A Secret 'Debt Wish'?

How we think tends to determine what we do, and in turn, what we do tends to determine the results we get. What do you catch yourself thinking on a regular basis? Do some of your thoughts have a *self-destruct* quality to them, some kind of 'debt wish' that does you no favours on the financial front?

What are some of the things you've told yourself about spending money and going into debt? Below are a few case-studies that paint a picture of some of the most unhelpful identities you can have as a problem spender. They demonstrate many of the ways in which people choose to define themselves through their relationship with money.

One or more of them might seem familiar to you. You might see shades of your best friend, your partner, or even yourself. Notice in particular how beliefs and values shape and define our identities. At the same time, try to figure out what kind of spender *you* might be.

Test Yourself: 5 Common Problem-Spender Identities

1. The Four-Wheel Drive Worth-ometer

It's easy to be dazzled by Brent. He has the opposite sex eating out of his hand. He dresses well. He drives fast cars. But all is not as it appears. Brent thinks he can buy approval on a monthly lease. His M-Class Mercedes looks the part, but it is killing him financially. Good thing that car is fast. Among many other obligations, Brent is still running away from his Council Tax payments of some years ago. At least the bailiffs can't repossess Brent's car: it isn't really his to begin with.

Despite his bluster, Brent actually has very little inherent self-worth. On some level he feels his background and upbringing have given him a bit of a raw deal in life, and he needs to make up for it in whatever way he can – at whatever cost.

2. Dirty Money

Money just seems to slip through Mandy's fingers. As soon as she gets it, it's gone – not because she is a reckless spender, but because she gives it all away. When Uncle Harry died, she got a five-figure windfall. She lent the money to her boyfriend. But they broke up, and she'll probably never see that money again. 'Oh that's okay, it's only money', she rationalises.

Britain's debt-collecting bailiffs were 70 per cent busier in 2005 than they were two years before, according to the 16 July 2006 Guardian. *Things don't always have to reach such a critical stage, but apparently these days more than half the calls made to debt advice centres go unanswered due to the high volume of enquirers.*

She frequently complains that the reason rich people stay rich is because they keep it all to themselves. 'They're the worst tippers.' And Mandy should know – she's been a waitress for nine years.

According to Mandy, wealthy people don't know how hard people have to *work* for their money in 'the real world'. That's why when the tables are turned, and Mandy is the one enjoying a meal out, she invariably leaves an over-generous tip: 'I'm not interested in being loaded,' she reasons. 'It's perfectly fine for me to live from month to month.'

The trouble is that being a waitress at 47 isn't as easy as it used to be. But she has to keep working, because she can't afford to pack it in and move toward something more suitable.

3. A Great Big Stack Of Love Coupons

Divorce is on the rise again, according to figures published by Payplan in 2008. Of 157,000 divorcing couples reviewed, the findings indicated that debt can even be the root cause of relationship breakdowns and divorce proceedings. It seems to be a case of 'til debt do us part'.

If you want to know more about how debt might be making your relationship a bit tricky, have a look at the website under **www.wealthmechanic.com/relationships**

Kenneth needs to be needed, and buying things shows his family and friends that he cares. He is forever helping his daughter and her husband out of financial jams – and not wanting to play favourites, he bought a car for his 27-year-old son who moved back home two years ago after completing university.

Every year for his wife's birthday, Kenneth spares no expense, and buys her gifts that cost several thousand pounds. But his largess doesn't stop with the family.

Against his wife's better judgement, Kenneth lent $30,000 (£15,000) to his best mate Charlie, after he lost his job through redundancy. After all, what are friends for?

That's all well and good, but Kenneth finds he is in overdraft every month, despite a successful consultancy business and a six-figure income.

4. It's Better than Prozac

When she was growing up, Sally's mother always confided, 'There's nothing like a bit of retail therapy.' True to her word, Mum took Sally out for a bit of a jolly every Saturday afternoon.

Nothing has changed in 20 years, although Sally is now married, and has a little girl of her own. A few times a week, she nips out with her friends at work and buys something – even something small – during her lunch hour. 'We girls always have such fun when we go out together.' Sally loves the thrill of trying on clothes and shoes. And when she and the girls return to the office, they do a little fashion parade. 'Beats the heck out of Prozac,' she is fond of saying.

Stanford University Medical Centre recently found that more than 70 per cent of a group defined as 'compulsive shoppers' responded favourably to a prescribed antidepressant, as reported in the April 2006 edition of Fortune.

But as good as shopping makes Sally feel, it has been a source of strife at home. She's been starting to hide her purchases from her husband, Bob, who recently has been complaining that she is over-spending.

5. There's No Business like Show Business

It has always been Carmela's dream to be her own boss. Two years ago she formed a small company with some savings, after being made redundant on the eve of her thirtieth birthday.

Pitching her tent as a freelance marketing consultant, Carmela always aims high, and when it came to the company there were no holds barred; she spared no expense. Anxious to make the right impression, she opened a showy office in the nice part of town.

She soon had a receptionist, a part-time assistant, a fancy phone system with intercoms, stunning business cards, a website, top-of-the-range computers, and even a twelve-seater conference room. Carmela saw it this way, 'You have to look the part, don't you? Otherwise nobody will take you seriously.'

And who knows? Had those fancy phones been ringing a little bit more often, Carmela might have eventually been in the money. But, as it was, she used up all her savings, took out a second mortgage, and found herself paying the receptionist's wages on her credit card. In the end, Carmela had to let her staff go, and now has her office in a spare room at home.

Owners of small- and medium-sized enterprises in the UK are spending an astonishing £1.8 billion a month on their personal credit cards to help fund their ventures, cited research by the Warwick Business School.

Nick Hood, of business-rescue firm Begbies Treynor, commented, 'The chances are that a large slice of that £1.8 billion was spent by relatively few companies. Many of them will have been startups, still trying to establish a track record,' according to a 27 June 2005 article in Startups.

We *All* Get Hold Of Some Funny Ideas – Not Just You

You may see shades of yourself in any one of these people. You may be trying to look the part, in the same way as Brent. You may feel just as trapped as Mandy, in a job that you no longer enjoy. You may be starting to hide your purchases from your partner, just as Sally finds herself doing.

At the core of all these stories lies more than one kind of fear: Carmela has a deep-seated fear of dependence; Kenneth harbours a fear of *in*dependence. Brent is showing his fear of failure; and Mandy carries a fear of success.

At the height of my own particular days of spending madness, my biggest fear of all was being 'rumbled'. You see, I believed that if my friends figured out I wasn't on an equal financial foothold, they wouldn't want to hang out with me any longer. This self-limiting belief drove me to mismanage my credit cards, so I could live up to an image I had created for myself.

Brooklyn's Very Own 'Poster Boy' For The Galatea Effect

So what are the top three beliefs that generate the highest degree of fear when *you* fix your gaze on your overall financial situation? I invite you to write them down on a separate piece of paper before you read on. Afterwards, take a good look at what you've written down, and select the belief that seems to generate the most fear of all.

At this point it shouldn't surprise you that many of us get hold of some funny ideas about what money can and cannot bring into our lives. We usually don't even realise we have them, but they've got us under some kind of spell. It's all a bit unconscious. That's the right word for it: UN-conscious; NOT conscious. This is why it is important to have a look at what kind of problem spender *you* might be. But that's hard to do, because most of us are asleep at the wheel.

The amount of business-related debt is seen as an increasing problem in the UK. Nearly one in every five UK companies regards their levels of debt as the biggest threat to their survival.

In October 2005, Colin Haig of PricewaterhouseCoopers commented, 'Rising levels of corporate debt and low levels of consumer spending are twin perils facing struggling British business. We are seeing lots of companies who are already showing signs of distress.'

Until we take a good look at ourselves, it probably wouldn't matter if, like Mandy, we inherited a windfall. Our perception of who we are in relation to money would remain the same.

Without ridding our lives of unhelpful beliefs about who we are, it's likely we'd somehow manage to find a way back to reduced circumstances all over again.

Spending on handbags was found to have more than doubled in five years, according to a survey by the market researchers Mintel. Less than half the group surveyed owned fewer than ten of them.

Tamara Mellon, owner of the Jimmy Choo label, offered an explanation in the 17 March 2006 Telegraph, 'For women of all ages and from all walks of life, acquiring a handbag is an enjoyable experience, a mood-altering exercise.'

In this same article, a Prudential study found that the average handbag contained around £550 (more than $1,000) worth of personal possessions.

A lot of us would probably just keep doing what we're doing, except we'd just keep doing *more* of it – though for a while there would be more noughts on our bank statement entries.

Let's learn a lesson from Mike Tyson, perhaps Brooklyn's most famous story of rags-to-riches-to-rags. Declared the undisputed world heavyweight champion at the age of 21, Tyson found incredible wealth and fame at an early age.

Nevertheless, some years ago he filed for bankruptcy after burning through more than $300 million, and being forced to sell his 48,000-square-foot Connecticut mansion. After losing his home, Tyson revealed, there were times when he had to sleep in homeless shelters and live on handouts.

His devastating self-assessment at the age of 38 spoke volumes: 'My whole life has been a waste. I am a failure,' he was quoted as saying. As a successful heavyweight boxer, he was known throughout the world as 'Iron Mike', with tremendous potential within the sport. Yet when he looked at himself in the mirror, he saw a 'failure', and perhaps he did whatever it took to make it all come true.

Get Under The Hood And Retrain Your Brain

The mind is powerful, and on some level your thoughts *do* determine your destiny. So be vigilant in regard to what you allow yourself to think. It is powerful and enlightening when you start to connect the dots between the various beliefs that hold you back and the emotions that link up to them. But the awareness of these connections counts for nothing unless you somehow *apply* whatever has begun to hit home.

So, start to 'retrain your brain' today: it's not very helpful to hold onto the idea that you don't deserve money, that you'll never have enough of it, and that you wouldn't be able to manage it effectively if you did. And be especially careful with the stories you choose to tell yourself – good or bad, they often have a tendency to surprise you by coming true. In the next chapter, we are going to look at the damaging effects of worry and anxiety – and how the right experience of 'fear' can actually be the best thing that ever happens to you.

THE NUTS AND BOLTS OF THIS SECTION

☞ How you think determines what you do, and what you do determines the results you get

☞ So many of us are 'asleep at the wheel' because we consistently act from within fear-based thinking

☞ Many of us hold onto unconscious ideas about what 'money' can and cannot bring into our lives

☞ Without ridding yourself of unhelpful beliefs about who you are, you tend to revert to longstanding and often destructive habits

☞ The beliefs that hold you back are usually tied to a set of 'stories' you have convinced yourself to be true

CHAPTER 9

FASTEN YOUR SEATBELT
What we'll be covering this trip...

☞ Realise when limited thinking stops you from getting what you want

☞ Beware when fear fools you into believing it is something else

☞ Understand the essential difference between 'healthy fear' and worry or anxiety

☞ Make the link between what you focus on and what you achieve

☞ Discover the one thing that will neutralise feelings of fear, doubt and shame

☞ Recognise when you choose to think and behave in a certain way, even when it hurts you

"Ultimately we know deeply that the other side of every fear is freedom"
Marilyn Ferguson

The battle is always won or lost in the way we view a particular situation: we can choose to emphasise what is wrong with our lives, or we can decide to focus on what is right. External events don't determine our happiness, but internal attitudes most certainly do. You may have fears and doubts about any number of things, but here's something I know about you at this very moment: you've likely got a place to sleep tonight; you've got some clothes to wear; and your next meal is sorted. Who could ask for anything more, right? All of your essential needs are being met, even if your home is hardly Shangri-la.

When obsessing about how bad it is, you probably tend to forget what's good. The nice stuff just doesn't fit the story you keep telling yourself. It is important to maintain a sense of perspective. You may not have everything you want, but it's a giant leap to pretend that you have nothing – or that everything you've bought on credit has someone else's name on it.

No Need To Slam The Door On *Your* Promising Future

Try not to convince yourself that you're the only person for miles who feels this way. A whole lot of people out there feel constrained by what they lack. When they focus on their finances, it is within the context of what they *don't* have, rather than what they *do*. Many people – not just you – often feel trapped by their debts, and they blankly stare into the distance as if they were standing on the wrong side of the bars of a prison cell.

Don't get me wrong, your debts are very real indeed – but those 'iron bars' are most definitely not! Each so-called bar is something you've chosen to believe, or as a direct consequence of your beliefs, is something you've chosen to *do* or to *feel*.

You don't have to bend the bars with superhuman strength to set yourself free – you just have to slide open the door of your 'cell' and walk across the threshold. It will surprise you how *powerful* you begin to be when you step outside the prison of limited thinking. But if you keep kicking yourself for being a so-called failure, there is no way you can step forward and start making some long-lasting changes.

So what's actually stopping you (or anybody else) from living a life of prosperity, freedom and abundance... starting tomorrow? Limited thinking is often difficult to recognise and name, but when we are able to shine a light on it, we begin to see that often this is precisely what keeps us from getting what we want out of life – and it can also prevent us from enjoying what we already have.

Fear Is The 'Chameleon' Of All Human Emotions

From my experience as a psychotherapist, I realise that nearly all of us have deep-seated fears about money, but we usually keep these feelings well under wraps. It's not easy to admit that we have such fears, but it is *especially* difficult to admit the presence of fear to ourselves.

The trouble is that fear is the 'chameleon' of all human emotions; fear often fools you into thinking it is an entirely different kind of sensation. You see, many of us learned from an early age that fear was a 'no-go' form of expression. In order to avoid exposure, we might have learned to portray 'fear' as anything but! How about anger? Arrogance? Placid but false serenity? Resignation? Helplessness? Or depression? And if a strategy gets us results from an early age, what would ever call it into question years down the line?

So the first thing to do if you are ready to confront some of your fears is to make sure 'fear' isn't masquerading as something *else*. Thankfully, it is easier than you might imagine to remove the mask – to verify that what you are experiencing is genuine fear. When it's the real deal, it actually inspires and motivates you to take action. That's why I tend to call it 'healthy fear'. *Healthy* fear? Have you ever grabbed hold of a toddler's arm just before she tugged on a pot of boiling hot water? Or slammed on the brakes when somebody in front of your car comes to a sudden stop? It happens entirely by instinct, doesn't it?

Worry and anxiety don't tend to mobilise our resources in the same way as healthy fear. Instead, these particular sensations have a habit of inducing a state of near-paralysis. Rather than serving as a 'call to arms', worry and anxiety tend to steer us away from acting on the get-up-and-go sensation we access through healthy fear.

What if you suddenly realised that you were about to bounce a cheque, one that would be particularly embarrassing? Healthy fear might get you sprinting down to the bank during your lunch hour in order to arrange a hasty transfer from another account. But longstanding anxieties about 'the sorry state of your finances' might mean you avoid things by talking yourself into having a pub lunch, followed by a spot of window-shopping instead. If so, you exist in a general state of unease, rather than being motivated by healthy fear. In such a situation, it can help you to face the fear head-on by asking:

- What is it that I am *actually* avoiding or putting off?

- Does naming *what it really is* motivate me to take any particular action?

Healthy Fear: The Fuel That Actually Propels Your Success

If you were unable to pinpoint a particular action you would be compelled to take, you might not have succeeded at getting in touch with the sensation of healthy fear. When that's the case, try looking at things from a different perspective. If, on the other hand, you had the strong sense that what you were exploring was indeed healthy fear, the realisation would be accompanied by a motivation to *do* something – to *act* on it. After all, the 'fear' itself might scare you out of your wits, but this isn't half as bad as the paralysis that so often arises when one of our other emotional expressions is masquerading as fear.

It is certainly easy for me to encourage you to face your fears head on. After all, I've already been where you are now. Hindsight has taught me that, more often than not, only one thing stands between success and failure with this stuff. And it isn't ever the *absence* of fear that empowers us, but the determination to peer into the darkness, no matter how scared we are. Without healthy fear, it would be impossible to experience what it actually means to be brave. Indeed, healthy fear is the fuel that propels us toward a place of genuine courage.

Once Things Are Moving, Keep Your Eye On The Road

My Mum taught me how to drive a car, and I am happy to say that she survived the experience intact. It was a bit of a white-knuckle ride at times, and I *was* the lucky one – I had the steering wheel to hold on to!

She told me one thing I've never forgotten because the wisdom of it applies to all of life. As I'd veer toward the hard shoulder she'd warn, 'Look at where you want to go, not where you *don't* want to go.' What she meant was that a car tends to follow our gaze. And that is true with the rest of our lives as well: what you focus on is what you will tend to achieve, the direction you will follow.

Once you define your goals, set your sights on the road ahead – and not on the journey you've just taken. In other words, focus on the possibilities of the future, not the limitations of the past.

You Can Fix It... You Can... You Can... You Can

A lot of us try to take the part of our lives we fear the most, and keep it at arm's length. Somehow we think that if it recedes into the shadows, it doesn't really exist anymore. Out of sight, out of mind.

The truth is that when, instead, we actually have the courage and the resolve to face our biggest fears – hold them close to our chest – only then do we begin to slay the monsters. Avoiding your fears doesn't make them go away. Facing them doesn't give them more power.

So how do you actually feel, in the pit of your stomach, about money itself? If you are like most people, on some level you feel afraid, but perhaps you can't quite put your finger on it –

no matter how many noughts you have on the end of your bank balance. Either you are concerned that you're lacking in funds at the moment, or you are worried that there won't be enough around the corner. Here's the problem: the harder you try to push such fear into the shadows, the more it rears its ugly head. In fact, you can burn a lot of calories pushing this kind of fear into the nether reaches of your mind. It is far more positive to face your fears, which is the first step toward changing your beliefs about who you are.

When it comes to 'money' it's not always easy to think in terms of what it really is. We concentrate on what money can buy rather than what it can do. As a result, this makes it easy to think about the value of things rather than the feelings they generate.

I know firsthand how much it takes to face your fears. It requires a lot to steer yourself headlong into each and every financial and emotional challenge coming your way. Trust that 'who you are today' is who you're meant to be. But at the same time, you somehow need to swerve around the limitations of the present, and look toward the road ahead.

A brighter future for *you* is out there somewhere – squint your eyes, peer through the darkness, and have faith in the light of your own courage and conviction, however faint it might be at this stage. It often helps to remember that sometimes what we fear is so hidden that what lurks in the shadows isn't half as bad as we imagine it to be.

Okay, maybe your debt dilemma looms larger than life. If so, you're not alone. Welcome to the club… yes, it's *your* problem and nobody else's. You are the one who can take charge of it – not the credit card companies, your partner, your boss, the economy or the Government. And *yes,* you can fix it. You can. You can. You can.

You Are *Not* Your Bank Balance

Just because you might think you've messed up somewhere along the way, it doesn't mean you are obliged to feel bad about yourself forevermore. Though it's sometimes hard to believe, you are not your bank balance – and you are definitely not your debts.

The next time you get a late-evening telephone call from one of your credit card companies, or a nasty letter from a debt collector, it would be good if you quietly reminded yourself of that. They can't just show up and take a pint of your blood, or cart away your first-born son. Debtors' prison went out of fashion way back in the 19th Century. You may owe someone money, but you don't owe them your life and soul.

Many people hang onto limited beliefs about the money they owe, and such beliefs can hold them back year after year. I hold the view that, on some level, what each of us has long ago decided to believe about 'money' determines how much of it we actually have in the bank. The problem arises when we become stuck in a certain emotional stance, and that position either enables us to have what we deserve and to keep it, or it prevents this from happening as fully as possible.

Debt's Just Like A Flat Tyre: It Can Be Fixed

You may feel as if you are in a state of complete paralysis, and that your life won't begin again until you get your debts behind you. But in order to apply the mindset of the Wealth Mechanic programme successfully, you'd need to hold to the view that your circumstances are fixable, and in that sense *temporary* – provided that you take the right steps.

It's difficult to imagine you can 'fix your finances' when there's an underlying sense of self-blame, but please don't fall into that trap. There is *no* blame involved here. You didn't plan it this way, and you don't deserve to be punished. Debt is a situation. It's *temporary*. Like a flat tyre, it is something that can be fixed.

The best way to begin to neutralise any feelings of fear, doubt or shame is to take action. These sensations are telling us that we would do well to make some serious changes, either to how we are choosing to behave or to what we are choosing to believe – and typically such change is required on *both* fronts!

The problem is that some of our emotions can act as powerful and restrictive 'financial roadblocks', and these can introduce barriers to happiness, wealth and prosperity. Our forward journey can so easily come to a screeching halt when we continue to carry at our side the heavy burdens of fear, doubt and shame.

When we are in debt, these deep-seated feelings can easily keep us from taking actions that move us closer to the freedom we want to bring into our lives. Have you ever heard yourself saying anything similar to the following?

- **My financial affairs are in such a terrible state that I can't face dealing with them, so I'm better off stashing my post in a box, unopened – at least until the end of the month.'** (A belief tinged with a sense of fear, and one that acts as a financial roadblock).

- **I don't suppose I could *ever* make any headway at this late stage, so I'll just keep doing what I've been doing.'** (A belief tinged with a sense of doubt, and one that acts as a financial roadblock).

- **I'm so ashamed about this. I would be ruined if anyone ever found out, so I'm not going to make any calls to see what help there is out there.'** (A belief tinged with a sense of shame, and one that acts as a financial roadblock).

Inner Voice Thinking: The Fork In The Road

Without a doubt, the sensations of fear, doubt and shame can boldly colour what you choose to do – or not to do – on a day-to-day basis. When these particular feelings cause you to act in a way that is self-defeating, it could be said that *they* hold the purse strings, not you. But once you shine a light on the self-limiting beliefs that brought such emotions into being, you can change the course of your financial future once and for all.

Sometimes we get the greatest benefits in life when we 'think outside the box'. The first forward move is to stop being ashamed of the content of your issues.

Just be glad you're finding a way to view things from a different perspective. When there's pain of some kind we all find a coping-strategy, a pattern that keeps it all together.

If you have taken anything to heart from these last few chapters, I hope you will realise this: on some level we actually *choose* how we think and, in turn, how we behave – even when our thinking and our behaviour hurt us. And life has a tendency to unfold in a way that directly reflects those choices. Along the way, many obstacles are put in our path – but even in *these* moments we can decide how to deal with what is happening.

The key is to start making courageous decisions that fuel what we actually want to get out of tomorrow... and to avoid making choices that only serve to stall the engine.

Here are some examples of 'inner voice' thinking, depending on whether a person decides to be mired in fear or uplifted by courage. Notice which side of the column most closely resonates with the sort of voice you tend to hear whispering inside your own head:

Fear-based thinking:	**Courage-based thinking:**
I have a sense of nothing but lack in my life	I expect nothing but the very best for myself
I carry a great deal of envy toward some people I know of	I am exactly where I'm supposed to be, right at this point in time
I am feeling very down about things	I am optimistic about the future

If You Always Take The Easy Route, Life Is *Never* Easy

Sometimes it takes a surprising amount of courage to commit to choices that serve you in the best way possible, especially in the presence of a great deal of fear. There's no escaping this – as a matter of fact, nearly every decision you will make in life is grounded in either fear or courage. Part of you, perhaps on a semi-conscious level, is forever taking notes on whether you are holding yourself back or putting your best foot forward. I encourage you to enhance this ability and use it more deliberately. And yet it is difficult to accept that you might firstly need to glance in the rear-view mirror and lock eyes with the faces of fear and courage simultaneously. If you are only willing to do what is easy, life will tend to be difficult. When you are willing to do what's difficult, life often becomes amazingly easy.

Success isn't ever about avoiding our problems. None of us wants to believe it, but the only time we are actually *growing* is when we're feeling uncomfortable. Thus it is through confronting our fears, not avoiding them, that powerful results unfold – and that's precisely where we are heading as we move onto the next section.

THE NUTS AND BOLTS OF THIS SECTION

☞ When most people focus on their financials, they see what they *don't* have, rather than what they do

☞ Limited thinking often keeps you from getting what you want and enjoying what you already have

☞ 'Healthy fear' is accompanied by a get-up-and-go response; worry and anxiety have the opposite effect

☞ It isn't the *absence* of fear that empowers you and brings you success, but the determination to face it

☞ Some of your emotions act as financial 'roadblocks' that introduce barriers to wealth and prosperity

Redefining Your Forgotten Dreams

Many years ago, a very wise and special person urged me to live life with a sense of possibility rather than seeing it as hampered by limitation. My friend Josephine is now in her late-80s. She has been an inspiration and mentor since my childhood. And she never stops.

Decide What You *Really* Mean By Prosperity, Freedom And Abundance

Josephine still goes on archaeological digs, serves as a trustee for various organisations, volunteers for charity, and always seems to be learning to play another musical instrument. She continues to be an inspiration.

I would never have guessed that a simple outing with Josephine when I was a young lad would have had such an impact on my life. One sunny California day, Josephine decided to take me to an antiques emporium, but when we arrived it was shut. Undaunted by this turn of events, she peered through the window and enquired, 'Max, if you could have anything in there, *anything* at all, what would you choose?'

'Nothing,' I stammered.

She sighed, 'Oh c'mon, Max. Try again.' She waited to see if I would rise to the occasion. Frustrated, I told her I thought it was a stupid game, a bit of torture, to even consider such a question – since I obviously couldn't afford a single thing within those four walls.

Josephine stooped down, looked me straight in the eye and said, '*I'm* talking about possibilities – and *you're* talking about limitations. Never live your life that way. Not even for a day. It's a big mistake.' She then asked me if a university degree with my name on it might be on the cards.

> **If you don't have something to aim for, believe me, you've got nothing**

'Gimme a break,' I thought to myself. 'That's a long way away.' But after a long pause, I finally whispered, 'Dunno…I'm only ten years old.'

I could sense Josephine's impatience as she rested her hands on my shoulders. She then looked me squarely in the eyes and gave me what-for: 'Listen to me carefully, Max. However you do it, you've got to start to broaden your horizons, *right* now. You've got to imagine the *possibilities*. The academic world isn't for everyone; that I know. But it opened a lot of doors for me, and I can't help but think it'd do the same for you. Just because you're young, it doesn't mean you can't dream about what the future holds.'

Josephine then softened toward the startled little boy, who by now was instinctively standing at attention: 'It's just that clearly you need something up your sleeve that makes you believe you can do anything – absolutely *anything*. Even when you're an old man, you need to keep hold of a dream or two. From now until the day you die, if you don't have something to aim for, believe me, you've got nothing.'

I have never forgotten that moment. It is etched in my brain to this day. No matter what happens to me in life, it always colours my thinking: always aim for *something*, and always imagine

When you have a bit more than you need, it creates possibilities

the possibilities. Admittedly, sometimes the possibilities seem at low ebb when you feel that you don't have what you want or need – or when debt overshadows every aspect of your life. The key to *genuine* happiness is a sense of balance... and a healthy dose of the sensations of prosperity, freedom and abundance; is part of this.

And it isn't always what's in your wallet that determines the strength of these sensations. We've all heard of people who have everything they could *ask* for but are desperately unhappy. Indeed, what can money actually buy? What is the point of accumulating wealth, if you don't choose to enjoy it or to share it sensibly?

Ask any lottery winner what it meant to them when all those noughts suddenly appeared on their bank statement. For some people, I suppose the thought alone triggers images of briefcases brimming with cash, guitar-shaped swimming pools, and cars I'd be too embarrassed to drive. There's nothing wrong with that. I'm glad somebody's revelling in it somewhere out there at this moment.

But money in itself only ever 'buys' you one of two things. When you have a bit more than you need, it creates possibilities. When you have a bit less than you need, it creates limitations. It reminds me of what Mr Micawber said in Charles Dickens' *David Copperfield*: 'Annual income twenty pounds, annual expenditure nineteen nineteen and six; result: happiness. Annual income twenty pounds, annual expenditure twenty pounds ought and six; result: misery.' Indeed, if 'prosperity, freedom and abundance' prove to be nothing more than positive feelings – upbeat sensations – then each of us could choose to invoke these feelings in our lives every day, *starting today*.

In that sense, I hold the view that prosperity in itself isn't the answer to anything in particular. At best it's a tool, something you can use to create the kind of life you want to put into motion for yourself and your family. At its most basic level, money is part of the machinery of life. And discovering a way to keep more of it in my *own* pockets was the launching pad of the Wealth Mechanic programme.

When I was heavily in debt, I was forever constrained by my own limitations. The balance of my life was skewed. At the time, I was choosing to believe that, before I could explore possibilities, I had to completely climb out of the financial hole I had fallen into.

So, has my own particular race to the financial finish line affected the course of my life thus far? Yes! There really is such a thing as 'life after debt'. Do you remember way back in the first few pages of the book, when I described how I learned that 'freedom has its price'? In a way, *freedom* was what I bought when I applied myself to the strategies that evolved into the Wealth Mechanic programme – the freedom to reconstruct my life the way I wanted to lead it.

The freedom I fought for and won gave me the opportunity to rehabilitate some long-forgotten dreams. Although I had worked so hard to be a successful architect, I was no longer finding it a fulfilling career. I'd begun to suspect that I could contribute more through retraining as a psychotherapist – a decision that still enriches my life to this day.

Because of the Wealth Mechanic strategies, I developed new-found confidence – and thus I believed in myself enough to take a few chances. My leap of faith took an unexpected direction: a friend of mine and I decided one day to live out a commonplace fantasy by opening a restaurant around the corner. Although I had no prior experience, part of me simply wanted to see if I could do it – and do it well.

Being my own boss was an extraordinary and rewarding adventure. Nonetheless, some six years down the line, I started to feel I'd fully extracted all there was to learn from the experience – and we sold it as a successful going concern.

The point is, we *did* it – and isn't that what life should be about? After all those years of getting it so wrong financially, the experience enabled me to re-shape my self-belief and confidence afresh by finally getting something so right. I would never have had the opportunity to follow my dreams – explore life's possibilities – if I hadn't earned the financial freedom to take a few chances. Yes, freedom definitely has its price. But often it's a price worth paying – don't you agree?

CHAPTER 10

FASTEN YOUR SEATBELT
What we'll be covering this trip...

☞ Understand that awkward feelings are common to nearly every one of us

☞ Realise that changing your life involves a minefield of surprising risks

☞ Know that for many, time and relationships are worth more than money

☞ Discover a secret strategy that will almost 'scientifically' engineer your better future

☞ Connect the dots between your emotions and how you experience the world

"There is only one success: to be able to spend your life in your own way"

Christopher Morley

Words like 'prosperity', 'freedom' and 'abundance' conjure up completely different images for each and every one of us. Exploring what these terms mean from *your* particular perspective might be stepping into uncharted territory – especially if you have been living your life for a very long time within the mindset of poverty. In this chapter we shall take a very brief look at what it would mean to completely turn your back on negative thinking – and to permanently adopt a mindset of *prosperity*.

If uncomfortable feelings or cynical thoughts arise as you think about the notion of prosperity and whether you deserve it, just let them come. They frequently lurk in the shadows after many years of a financial struggle – in fact, you might discover that you've been harbouring negative feelings about wealth and prosperity for a very long time. Don't feel bad about it. It's very common.

Keep Your Compass Pointed In The Right Direction

Awkward feelings often emerge as you discover the life you truly want to lead, especially if you're coming from adverse circumstances. As an example, you may feel as if you don't actually deserve prosperity. The best way to overcome these awkward – often self-limiting – feelings is to simply keep your eye on the road.

Wherever that road takes you, keep your compass pointed in the right direction as you continue the journey. Learn to place more trust in your internal navigation system. After all, True North is True North everywhere.

Knowing where you are going is *one* thing, but it's not just the knowledge that gets you there. You need to have a few other things to hand. The good news is that none of these things costs any money – and you already possess each of them to some degree or another.

Energy, poise, self-belief, commitment, a clear picture of your aspirations, and the support of others will fuel your journey and ultimately bring you closer to a genuine sense of prosperity in your life. So what does it mean to be 'prosperous' in your eyes? Most of us think that if we had a lot more money we'd be a *lot* more sorted. Right?

Deep Down, Do You Fear Success More Than Failure?

Many a joke starts off like this: a man is walking along the beach when he comes across an odd-looking bottle. Not being one to ignore tradition, he rubs it – and much to his surprise, a genie appears.

'For releasing me from the bottle, I will grant you three wishes,' says the genie. The man is ecstatic.

But with a 'genie joke' there's always a twist to the tale. Nothing is ever as simple as it first appears.

What if a genie granted you *your* top three wishes? What would be the twist to that tale? What would happen if you won the 'rollover' jackpot this coming Wednesday? Would you move house? Would you quit your job? What would your neighbours say? How about your friends from work? And what about your extended family? Maybe they'd all 'take the mickey' out of you, you posh so-and-so. Even worse, behind closed doors they might envy your wealth or resent your position. Perhaps they'd be suspicious of you, and you might have to find ways of relating to a whole new batch of people.

The strategies in the Wealth Mechanic programme don't involve such sudden changes in circumstance – but the idea of permanently altering your life for the better deserves some thinking time.

Are *you* one of the many who are actually afraid of wealth and prosperity? And what specifically are you getting in touch with when you catch a glimpse of such fear? Do you perhaps carry some kind of deep-rooted suspicion of success? 'What? Are you kidding? Success? Wealth and prosperity? Lay it on me!' you're probably saying.

As it happens, *many* of us have a fear of being perceived by others as successful – but it's buried deep down inside of us. There's an underlying sense that somehow we shall eventually be found out, exposed as a 'fake'. Others of us fear that people will think we're putting on airs. Maybe it feels safer to keep things just as they are. Better the Devil you know...

Don't Tell Me You've Never Fantasised About It

What is the definition of the word 'prosperity'? The dictionary isn't much help here, is it? Well, we all know that money can't buy you love – but it could buy a fair bit of happiness, couldn't it? And the Wednesday night 'rollover' might allow it all to fall into place…

I have only ever met one person who *wouldn't dream* of winning the lottery. I'll call her Martha. She asked to work with me one-to-one for a number of months, and I was slowly getting to know a person whose ideals were sound, and whose life seemed complex but fulfilling. At first I thought she was in denial about prosperity. I protested, 'C'mon, are you kidding? Haven't you ever pretended what it would be like to win the jackpot?'

The London 2012 Olympic Games and Paralympic Games will be funded in part from some £2.2 billion (more than $1 billion) from Britain's National Lottery, according to a 7 July 2008 report issued by Camelot Group plc, its licensed operator..

'Never ever,' she assured me, 'not even just for fun. Having a big win might risk upsetting the happiness I've already got.' Indeed, Martha did seem happy. She loved her job working with the elderly as a nurse, and she had a great relationship with her husband. Why would she want to win the lottery? She had it all.

Martha explained that she had thought about it in great detail at one of our workshops, and she was absolutely *certain* it wouldn't make her one bit better off… But I wouldn't hold it against you if you were saying to yourself right now, 'Martha's definitely in denial; she just doesn't realise it. Who the heck does she think *she's* kidding?'

A Millionaire Is Loading Our Dishwasher

In the 2004 Christmas Eve Superdraw, Andrea Birkbeck saw Lady Luck shine on her to the tune of £5 million – yes, that's hardly peanuts: $10 million. But within weeks of her staggering win, many national papers reported that Andrea amazed her friends by returning to her job in a department store just outside of Margate.

Earning thousands a week in interest from her lottery windfall, she had missed the camaraderie and friendship of her £125-a-week post (that's a job paying $250 a week). Her friends obviously had more currency than all those noughts on her bank statement.

Andrea's not the only one. Sue Viking was reported to have bagged a million pounds in 2002, but she still works at a canteen in a Kilkenny fire station. Apparently when she decided to stay, the word around the station was, 'Can you believe we've got a millionaire loading our dishwasher?' But why would she leave a job she loved? In fact, while more than a quarter of lottery winners in the UK have since started their own businesses, the same proportion still works for somebody else.

You Don't Need To Buy What You Already Have

Then there are all the stories of lottery winners buying acres of land on the moon, herds of water buffalo, football clubs, helicopters, private jets and castles. (All true, apparently – and what's wrong with that?) But among the top ten benefits of a lottery windfall is said by winners to be the ability to spend more time with family and friends.

Whether you're willing to admit it or not, like everyone else, you crave relationships with other people – relationships that make you feel valued and nurtured. You like to feel important to somebody out there, and you are undoubtedly proud to be considered something of a friend to at least one other person.

In order for good relationships to truly flourish, they take time to develop and maintain. In the exercises I did with my client Martha, she re-affirmed that whatever makes us feel prosperous is personal and unique. For her it was all about relationships. As a nurse, and one half of a loving couple, she was very prosperous indeed. What would *having more money* give her that she didn't already have?

No two personal definitions of prosperity are the same, because we are all so different. The secret is to keep listening for the real answers when you ask yourself the same old questions about what you want out of life.

Locking Eyes In The Bathroom Mirror: Who's *That?*

I don't personally know anybody who has hit the jackpot on the lottery – but a lot of us know someone who's pretty well off, yet somehow fairly unhappy in life.

Before you can establish a healthier relationship with the world around you, you've got to learn to have a compassionate relationship with *yourself*. That's where the *really* hard work begins, but it's worth putting in the time. If you can do what it takes, you'll gain a friend for life: your true self.

A lot of people out there are chasing after more and more money – or more things that money can buy – thinking this will give them a sense of prosperity. They believe gunning for this goal makes perfect sense. Perhaps they feel certain that having 'more and more' is what happiness is all about.

In the back of our minds most of us know there's more to life than money. Don't get me wrong - I'll be the first one to cheer you on as you go for the rewards you want in life. But money

on its own won't give life a sense of purpose and meaning.
So why are some people driven to chase after it as though it
would?

Through working with a lot of people, and becoming more
intimately aware of what makes them tick, I think most of us
aren't chasing after the actual things money can buy. As I said
earlier, I think prosperity might be nothing more real than
an upbeat *feeling*. But maybe it's a feeling that you don't need
stashes of cash to experience. Maybe you just need a bit of
imagination.

Nothing Wrong With A Bit Of 'White Magic'

Now I'm going to invite you to do a series of exercises that will
surely generate a smorgasbord of feelings. Try to keep an open
mind as we now explore the mindset of a millionaire. These
techniques take a good deal of imagination and sometimes
a great leap of faith – but they are enlightening. At the very
least, they will release a spectrum of unconscious feelings in a
way no other exercise can match.

If you perform these little exercises on a regular basis, tapping
into the mindset of a millionaire becomes easy, and has the
ability to change your entire outlook on life. As you read this
next section, you might start to think I'm into magic spells or
something like that… Come to think of it, maybe I am.

Let me explain: some of the techniques and strategies for
wealth creation seem entirely 'out on a limb' at first glance, but
they are powerful. Sometimes a little bit of 'magic', so to speak,
does us a world of good.

When I first dabbled with these techniques, it was nearly
impossible to set aside my inner voice, a voice that was
screaming inside my head with cynicism and sarcasm. Don't

worry. After a couple of tries your own negative inner voice will definitely go silent, or at least be somewhat quieter.

Even If It Feels Unreal, It Feels *So* Good

If on a deep level you think of yourself as a person who is meant to be poor, you will fear poverty instead of inviting prosperity. If you've been struggling with debts, you'll tend to tap into this sort of worry and fear on a daily basis – and whatever becomes your consistent focus tends to be what comes into your life. If all this holds true, surely you'd want to eradicate the mindset of poverty in whatever way you can.

Once you make the decision to walk away from the mindset of poverty, you can certainly do a lot in your mind to reaffirm that position.

Next time you pay for something, vividly imagine that you have tens of thousands in the bank – far more than would ever be necessary to fulfil that particular obligation. It feels good, doesn't it? Even if it feels a bit unreal in that moment.

And now I need you to dig out your chequebook from the kitchen drawer or wherever you keep it, and dust it off.

Here's what I'd like to see you do: practice writing cheques and paying-in slips for tens of thousands – then hundreds of thousands – on dozens of cheques and slips. When you run out, ask your bank for a new set. If both your mind and your body can get comfortable with the idea of depositing that much money into your bank account and spending those kinds of sums, you'll start to be able to visualise yourself as a person with considerable wealth.

Now, if you were *actually* depositing and spending these kinds of sums, your bank statement transactions would have quite a few more noughts after them (and not the initials 'OD' for 'overdrawn'). So, let's take the process a step further; why don't you take a recent bank statement, and photocopy it a couple of times? Rearrange the numbers so that you show a statement that's actually tens of thousands of pounds in credit. Once you've got it the way you'd like to see it, photocopy the result and display it on your desk or your bathroom mirror. Every so often, you'll want to rearrange the figures again, showing ever more noughts on the balances, and steering impossibly far away from overdrawn amounts. When you visualise the possibilities, miracles can and do happen.

The Untold Story: Your Personal Path To Prosperity

Sums like that shouldn't just sit in the bank doing nothing, should they? Life is for living. I'd like to now invite you to form a concrete picture of the future you desire – by creating a collage of images that will continue to inspire you as it takes shape organically.

If you'd like to live in a certain part of town, take photographs of houses and streets in that particular area. If you've always wanted to go on certain holidays, use the Internet or send away for travel brochures, and get photographs of these destinations.

If there's a certain kind of architecture you find particularly uplifting, find images in lifestyle magazines, and cut out examples of your favourite interiors. Do you like historic country houses? Perhaps you prefer modern glass penthouses. It's easy to find

More than one in four travellers has made a life-changing decision while on holiday, according to Internet holiday firm ebookers.

As reported in the 14 March 2005 Daily Express, 10 per cent of those surveyed had proposed to their partner thanks to a romantic break. Another 10 per cent said they made the decision to move abroad or to change their career.

hundreds of images of your dream home if you focus on noticing them around you.

While you're at it, ask a friend who has a colour copier to do you a little favour: photocopy some large-denomination banknotes and perhaps enhance their size. Cut out the images for your collage, and set them aside as well. You can then sprinkle your collage with images of 'stacks of cash', so you can get used to the feel of having larger sums around you. Set up a folder or a basket where you can file this array of images, and start to compose them over time.

Nothing Like A Good Game Of Golf, Is There?

Now, here's the best part: if there are people in your life you'd like to share success with, take photographs of them – then superimpose them onto different parts of the collage. You might place yourself and a friend in a holiday brochure picture. You might create the image of yourself cooking lunch with friends as you overlook a panoramic view of your favourite city from within your penthouse flat.

Hang this collage on the wall – but if you are embarrassed, mount it behind your bedroom door so you can secretly look at it as you fall asleep each night. Nobody will be the wiser except maybe your partner – and this is a person who's supposed to be on your side.

When you start to get a sense of what sorts of cars, houses and fun possessions you are attracted to, why not be cheeky, and go have a look at them in the flesh? I'm serious. Book a test drive of an amazing sports car in your favourite colour. It's not illegal, believe me. Visit an estate agent or realtor, and ask to view one of the properties you've been admiring in the window. Head for Harrods, London's world-famous department store, and try out a set of high-performance golf clubs – right there in the middle of the fifth-floor showroom!

If you are confident that having these things in your life would make you feel good, then road-testing those feelings *today* is one of the fastest ways to go about putting things into place for tomorrow. Nobody will lock you up for it! This is all about getting ready for a brighter future. After all, 99 per cent of 'sharpening the saw' is about sharpening the senses. Therefore making your aspirations as multi-sensory as possible is something that starts to have a lot of mileage.

Begin to form a picture of your Personal Path to Prosperity today. This starts to blaze an emotionally-charged trail toward what you want out of life, in what might prove to be one of the fastest ways possible. Who knows?

Follow Your Route Map – Things Will Turn A Corner

Remember that our emotions – both good and bad – are never determined by life's circumstances themselves; they are entirely the result of our *interpretation* of what is happening. Unconsciously, everybody is 'inventing stories' about what things mean – and no doubt you are too.

Have you ever got up in the middle of the night and, bleary-eyed, seen a 'ghost' out of the corner of your eye as you headed toward the bathroom? The hair on the back of your neck stands on its end… Frozen momentarily in fear, you muster up the courage to flick on the light – only to discover that someone had simply flung a bathrobe over the door. More than a bit embarrassed, you chuckle to yourself, do your business and go back to bed.

So unless you're Ebenezer Scrooge, how do 'ghostly visitations' after midnight relate to your decisions about what *prosperity* means? It's all about interpretation. Here's what I mean: what would the purchase of a flash car cause you to experience emotionally? Or how about a nice chunky Rolex? Or paying for your children's education? Or a cool million in the bank?

Nothing; nada; zilch. The experience of *having* any of these things wouldn't give you *any* sort of feeling at all – until you 'filed them in your head' by deciding what they meant to you.

What, for example, would a Rolex on your arm represent to you? How would you see yourself *then*? Would it make any difference to how you presently feel about yourself? If so, you have gained a powerful insight. This is what makes the material world go round – and this is also the key to understanding what makes a lot of us tick. In the next chapter, we are going to deepen our discussion about the material world, and discover how our outlook from within such a frame of reference links inextricably to issues of self-worth and self-belief.

THE NUTS AND BOLTS OF THIS SECTION

☞ Knowing where you are going is essential, but you first need to form a clear picture of your aspirations

☞ Before you establish a healthier relationship with the world around you, you've got to do so with *yourself*

☞ Wealth on its own won't give your life purpose and meaning. People who 'chase the money' fail to recognise this

☞ Forming a picture of your future blazes an emotionally-charged trail toward what you want

☞ Emotions are never determined by circumstances; they are entirely the result of *interpretation*

CHAPTER 11

FASTEN YOUR SEATBELT
What we'll be covering this trip...

☞ Discover how 'freedom' is linked to how much money is in your wallet

☞ Pinpoint what gives your life purpose and meaning

☞ Learn how to be happy at the flick of a switch

☞ Understand why your craving for 'stability' might cause internal conflict

☞ Know why people can be hurtful when you follow your own path

☞ Consider the buried truths that might well be holding you back

> *"Ask yourself what makes you come alive and go do that, because what the world needs is people who have come alive"*
>
> **Howard Thurman**

I imagine you have realised by this stage that the psychology explored in the Wealth Mechanic programme isn't solely concerned with overcoming debt and creating wealth. It's about living a more stress-free life starting *right now*, not in the future. In this chapter, we are going to discuss briefly what it means to have a mindset of *freedom*. You see, many of us unknowingly spend much of our time from within the mindset of *limitation*, instead of leading a life where freedom is always in our sightlines.

So how in the heck does the notion of *freedom* relate to how much money you've got in the bank? When you act from within a mindset of freedom, everything is about possibility. On the other hand, a life lived within the mindset of limitation imposes restrictions on yourself. The principles and strategies outlined in the Wealth Mechanic programme give results because they underpin strategic plans with the resourceful mindsets explored throughout this book.

133

It is important to believe, like my mentor Josephine, that you *deserve* to enjoy life's journey every step of the way. Indeed you are unlikely to be as fulfilled in your life if you're hell-bent on the end-goal, and fail to appreciate what's happening today.

Grab Hold Of The Steering Wheel And Hold On Tight

Talk about having a passion! Some women spend three years shopping for the perfect shoes and handbag, according to a July 2005 survey by Churchill Home Insurance.

In fact, over a lifetime the average British woman spends nearly £32,000 ($64,000) on shoes, with 86% of those surveyed enthusing that they buy at least one pair each month. Furthermore, a third of this group have 25 pairs in their wardrobe at any one time... That's some hobby!

As I said at the beginning of this book, the first taste of freedom comes when you grab hold of the steering wheel and get going in the right direction. You have now created your own route map, and if you follow it your life will change. It *will*. It can't help but change. Nothing changes until you do, but when you change *everything* changes.

When you begin to address your financial woes, you replenish more than your bank balance; you're growing in self-respect. This in turn widens your perspective as your focus is directed increasingly outward. When you knock yourself out of your own particular reverie – after being asleep at the wheel for a very long time – you wake up and take notice of things that were there all along.

If you're struggling with debt, you have scant little time and energy to look outside yourself, other than keeping yourself above water. But when you become financially free, you get a more balanced perspective on your life. You're likely to rediscover some of the *other* freedoms you may have forgotten… or long ago set aside. You finally have the ability to get back in touch with some of your non-financial goals and aspirations.

You might now have the freedom to take an evening class, so you can change your job, increase your salary, or simply learn something new. Or you could jump at the chance to start a new business. That, or you could simply take the time to travel overseas – maybe for the first time in your life.

Embrace What's Already Available – Especially If It's Free

What gives *your* life purpose and meaning? For starters, what's your greatest passion? What? You don't *have* one? Hokum! What energises you? What makes you shine like a star? What has an almost 'spiritual' quality for you? What makes you part of the Bigger Picture? It doesn't need to have a larger-than-life quality. Is it your job? Your children? Your friends? Classic cars? A decent bottle of wine? *The Archers* on BBC Radio 4? It doesn't have to make sense to anybody else, but it has to *start* making sense to you.

The good news is that before you've actually *achieved* complete financial freedom, you can experience these passions in your present life. Once again, it's all about interpretation. How do you fully embrace what's already available in your life today? You are free to find something in your job that makes you feel engaged, challenged and interested. Maybe you can maintain a 'buzz' by doing the best job possible.

A third of all borrowers lie about the reason for taking out a loan. Two people in every five took out more than £10,000 ($20,000) above what they needed, with a quarter of those surveyed spending it on holidays and many intending to launch a business venture via their borrowing.

Research in March 2005 by independent comparison service uSwitch.com indicated that over half of those surveyed justified their little white lies by saying that they didn't think their loan would be approved if they told the truth.

Even if there's not much in your wallet, you are free to spend more time with your children and friends. You may not *own* a classic car, but you're free to visit motor clubs and shows throughout the entire country – all for the price of a rail ticket. There are plenty of good wines available that cost under a tenner... and tuning into *The Archers* requires nothing more than a flick of a switch. There is a lot of happiness in the offing; much of it is inexpensive – or even free.

All activity that drives us toward some sort of personal development – be it emotional, mental, physical or social – is essentially 'spiritual' in nature.

Spiritual values take shape when you are mindful of widening horizons, personal growth and wholeness. Anything that creates a greater sense of vision and understanding of the world we inhabit is an aspect of a spiritual journey.

Spirituality exists whenever we find ourselves struggling with the issue of how our lives fit into the grand scheme of things. We also get in touch with spirituality when we are motivated by values that suggest a meaning beyond what we can touch and see.

Here's An Idea You Might Find Hard To Swallow

You may be feeling the limitations of your life: you've got bills to pay, jobs to go to, people to look after. Fair enough. Almost everybody does. But it's up to you to decide what these things mean; you can view them as a dead-end or you can see them from a different, more positive perspective. It's up to you.

It is the *interpretation* of your responsibilities that makes the difference in how you view them. As a psychotherapist, I have observed that we can often just *decide* to be happy. It's as simple as that. This is an idea you may find hard to swallow, but I've seen it many times. If you can decide to be happy – no matter what is going on around you – then you are 100 per cent accountable for your own choices.

Why is it so hard for some of us to get in touch with naming the things that make us feel free? You might believe that having a passion or a dream – at least right *now* in life – is a bit self-indulgent, or even impossible. But is it? Most of us absent-mindedly defer our passions. Months go by. Then years. Then decades. Maybe eventually we decide it's 'too late'. But it's *never* too late.

Millions of over-25 year-olds are interested in returning to study, but according to Lifestyle Extra, fewer than fifteen per cent actually fulfil their dreams. In fact, more than half of those surveyed found the cost to be a huge barrier in a 2005 study by financial services provider Mint.

What would it be like to construct your life almost entirely around your passions? It would probably take a lot of drive and guts, wouldn't it? If you're like most people you'd have to make some changes, or let go of a few long-held myths about what precisely is holding you back – besides the lack of funds. By all means, proceed with caution, but you've got to put the key in the ignition first.

Sometimes You Have To Lose Something To Find Something

A bull market on the stock exchange can make us feel rich, and in such times we tend to save less and borrow more while spending more.

And somehow, when house prices are buoyant, we feel even better off. But, proposes Geoff Colvin in September 2008's issue of Fortune, 'We might find that living within our means and saving a little money isn't actually so bad'. .

As often as you can, be in touch with *who you really are* – then everything else will have a tendency to fall into place more naturally. In fact, more and more of us know people who've decided to discover who they are through a process known as 'downshifting'. Downshifters eventually walk away from high-powered careers in the City, move to somewhere like Bexhill-on-Sea, adopt a Springer

Spaniel for the kids, and open a second-hand bookshop within walking distance of their beach hut. It's a dream come true, and they love it even more than the kids do.

There are times in life when you've got to lose something in order to find something. To my mind, living the life you want to lead is worth more than having a whacking great pay cheque. You can't put a price on finding out what makes you feel free.

'That's all very well for some,' you might be muttering. You may think that placing your passions first and foremost would be a step too far right now. Maybe you prefer a bit of certainty. After all, this life of doubts and fears has been stressful for quite some time, and you're used to it. Unlocking the shackles and making a break for freedom – actually jumping head first into uncertainty – may seem a bit reckless.

Sure, we all crave some kind of stability, but on the other hand there is only one thing I'm certain of in this life: we shall all depart someday. That's right – we have all bought a one-way ticket. Aside from that, absolutely nothing is certain. Life is a biscuit-tin that is passed around the table only once, so don't just dip your hand in and grab any old thing – pick one of the chocolate ones if that's your favourite!

EDF Energy announced plans to launch the energy industry's first-ever trust fund to help vulnerable customers who are struggling to pay their utility bills. The 15 September 2008 announcement cited Citizens' Advice Bureau research that revealed a 47 per cent increase in the number of consumer credit debt problems and showed that a quarter of those surveyed were receiving treatment for stress or depression.

Are You Out Of Your Mind?

So what are the downshifters really doing? Are they running away from limitation, or are they actually sprinting *toward* freedom?

We all have doubts and fears, but no matter what, there are two things you should never be without: self-worth and self-belief. What you are seeking is the kind of self-belief that can withstand a healthy dose of uncertainty.

As you make dramatic changes in your life, you will find that some people will support you as you aim toward your goals, but that others inevitably won't. No doubt every downshifter has had someone say, 'Are you out of your mind? How could you give up a great job, and cut your pay cheque in half so you can go off and live on the coast?'

People can be somewhat hurtful about change at times. They have their reasons. Part of it is fear – fear of the changes they glimpse in you. However it would be a shame to silence your own voice in order that theirs can be heard. One of my mentors, Suzanna McInerney, once put it to me this way:

It is not easy to stand apart; not easy to be different; not easy to hold to your own truth. Regardless of whether others believe you have it wrong, it is the confidence in your own truth that you are seeking to find. Do not wear others' shoes; do not take the values of others and try to adapt them for yourself. Discover your own values, and be proud to walk with them. Be true to yourself – and be true to your truth.

This counsel, a gift to me years ago when I very much needed to hear it, applies equally to *you* if you are trying to live a life that fits into someone else's expectations. A life lived for others alone is the ultimate limitation – and it can eventually lead to bitterness, cynicism and disappointment.

You can always find compelling reasons to keep things exactly as they are for the time being. But waiting for the *perfect* moment to break free from limitation is like putting happiness on hold until you win the lottery. Most people cash in their one-way tickets to the afterlife before the perfect moment comes –

but you can experience freedom in an instant once you realise that you have a unique contribution to make, a set of talents and gifts that ought to be shared. If you want to be happy right now, simply start to be the person you were meant to be all along.

Knee-Deep In The Mindset Of Limitation

Without realising it, have *you* decided to be unhappy? Are you hiding your true feelings? Are you trying to protect something? Are you attempting to control somebody? Are you aiming to manipulate a situation? Maybe you're setting out to punish someone – or even to punish *yourself*. If any of these things is true for you, ask yourself if perhaps you're knee-deep in the mindset of limitation.

Let's see if you can discover some of the ways you might have been holding yourself back in a given situation – or why you have colluded in the habit of keeping things exactly as they are.

What follows is an activity that I like to share with my clients, but you can do it by yourself in front of a mirror, or with a trusted person. Whichever way you decide to do it, try to set aside some time when you won't be interrupted or distracted. Either look straight at your own reflection, or face the person you have decided to pair up with, and complete both these declarations:

- 'I have decided to pretend that _____.'

- 'Actually, the truth of the matter is _____.'

Here are a couple of examples of what you might be saying: 'I have decided to pretend that I need to stay in this job for the sake of the children. Actually, the truth of the matter is I feel too old to retrain and look for a new job.'

On the other hand it might be something that is entirely contained within your view of yourself: 'I have decided to pretend that I enjoy living on a shoestring. Actually, the truth of the matter is I never thought I could amount to more than this.'

This exercise may go on for quite some time… and you may be surprised to hear what is coming out of your mouth. Just start the sentence off, and see what comes out. Time after time, much of what is buried deep in your subconscious tends to come to the surface. It also might be helpful to write down these revelations on paper.

When you have exhausted the process completely, it's good to reflect on the fundamental theme or themes. What did you discover about yourself? How many of these discoveries relate to the mindsets of freedom and limitation? What did it feel like to discover your own truths? And finally, what can you decide to *do* about them, now that they have been given a voice?

America's so-called HENRYs (High Earners; Not Rich Yet) are said to be the steam engine of the entrepreneurial and professional class that drives the American economy. According to the 20 November 2008 issue of Fortune, *HENRYs earn more than 98% of American households against a median income of $50,000 (£25,000) but aren't 'rich' either in terms of net worth or the ability to stop working and live on interest earned from savings and investments.*

When you don't feel 'free' in a situation – whether in terms of your finances or in any other area of your life – ask yourself, 'What am I *really* doing?' The answers can surprise and liberate you.

But It's Ever So Cosy In The Fur-Lined Rut

Here's a question for you: if it's so simple to become debt free and eventually well-off, how come everybody in the country isn't putting some sort of debt-recovery plan into motion? The fact is that a lot of people find things fairly tolerable just the way they are. It's tempting to stay in what is known as the fur-lined rut.

Many people settle into their feelings of limitation in a way that eventually seems familiar and comfortable. They never quite find the few minutes a day it takes to set something like the Wealth Mechanic programme into motion. They think it sounds too good to be true: 'Personal Path To Prosperity', my backside.'

On the other hand, maybe they were really into the idea for a while; they devoured this book from cover to cover – then put it on the bookshelf without really digesting the key points. You've heard the expression 'knowledge is power', but in this case knowledge counts for nothing. *Action* is what counts. All it takes is a little bit of effort, day after day. You'd hardly blow a gasket doing the Wealth Mechanic programme.

Britain is apparently the fifth most contented nation in the world. But not everyone loves their job, it seems. Two-thirds of British office workers eat lunch at their desk, and according to the 24 December 2005 edition of The Week, *a quarter of them are too scared to take a full lunch hour in case the boss disapproves.*

Slung Onto The Scrapheap: The Best-Laid Plans

Maybe you have put one or two of the principles of a *better mindset* into practice already. If so, I applaud you. If not, I suggest you take the handbrake off and put it into gear. This psychology isn't difficult to understand or to put into place. You just have to *start*.

It's wonderful to have the freedom to do what you love, rather than what you have to do in order to survive. For that reason, I really hope that *you* won't be one of those who will just read this book and put it on the shelf – without somehow *applying* the material between the front and back covers. You have taken your first major step by reading this far... please don't waste that effort.

Before we move on to the final chapter, it would be a good idea to go back to whichever section of the book made you stop and think about yourself the most. Where did you feel the most discomfort? Where did you get excited? Where did you skip a few pages because your *present mindset* made you believe that you couldn't handle it?

At the end of the day, whichever of the stops along the 'road to prosperity' most struck you, the final chapter of *Under The Hood* is meant as a potent reminder that the 'Galatea Effect' can make or break any sound strategy; preserve or spoil the most earnest intentions; and bolster or crush the best-laid plans.

THE NUTS AND BOLTS OF THIS SECTION

☞ Many of us spend much of our time from within the mindset of *limitation* instead of freedom

☞ When you address your financial woes, you replenish so much more than just your bank balance

☞ Whatever gives you purpose and meaning doesn't need to be larger-than-life or make sense to anybody

☞ Sometimes living the life you want to lead is worth more than a whacking great pay cheque

☞ People can be hurtful when you embark on a path of personal change. Don't silence your voice so theirs may be heard

CHAPTER 12

FASTEN YOUR SEATBELT
What we'll be covering this trip...

☞ Understand what the mindset of 'abundance' means

☞ Recognise the ways you have denied yourself since falling into the debt trap

☞ Discover how to adopt the mindset of a millionaire

☞ Realise that doing things for others can do a lot of things for you

☞ Beware the 'Golden Rule' when it comes to making a contribution

> *"Too many people are thinking of security instead of opportunity; they seem more afraid of life than of death"*
>
> **James F Byrnes**

The best-kept secret of success is the science of mindset. The right mental attitude can bring abundance into our lives, making it not only inevitable but unstoppable. In this final chapter, we are going to take a brief look at what it means to have a mindset of abundance. The world we live in tends to focus on lack, rather than abundance. When contrasted against most people's notion of prosperity, this sense of completeness is an entirely different idea.

Inherent to the notion of abundance is the awareness that happiness, by and large, arises solely from within; it is determined by how we look at our lives and interpret the ongoing events within them. When we trust that there is always enough to go around for us to have our fair share, we turn our back on the mindset of scarcity – an attitude that so often colours a life of financial struggle.

Yet so many people have a sense of scarcity and lack within their lives. Why do you suppose that is? Again, our attitudes and beliefs are either our worst enemy or our greatest asset.

To illustrate a small part of what I mean by this idea, I'd like to introduce you to Roger. His is a classic example of how the mindset of scarcity can sometimes pervade our lives in a way that's unhelpful to the extreme.

Ditch The 'Bunker Mentality' Once The War Has Ended

Britons spend £1.6 billion a year ($3.2 billion) on birthday celebrations. Jerry Toher, Managing Director of financial services provider Mint summarised their March 2006 survey with this observation, 'Close to a third of people said they used their birthday as an excuse to celebrate, and it's clear they're looking for something more than a cake and a few candles.'

Roger was only a young lad when Churchill announced on the radio that World War Two had ended. We all know that things were a bit lean for many years, both during the war and after it ended; but in Roger's mind those tough times never abated.

His wife Lois passed away a number of years back. She was smart enough to plan and pay for her own funeral. You see, she knew perfectly well that Roger had never been one to spend on frivolities. Go out for dinner? Only for birthdays and anniversaries. Wine at the restaurant? What's wrong with a jug of water? Just try to get Roger to go out for a pint without a reason! And every Christmas and birthday the grandchildren, now teenagers, would get an envelope with just one crisp fiver inside.

After Lois died, Roger was reduced to living on one state pension, and he felt that he had better cut corners a bit more. He actually stopped using dishwashing liquid to wash his dishes: 'Just use hot water from the kettle.' He didn't even bother with soap powder to wash his clothes: 'Stick 'em in the tub with a squirt of shampoo.' That saved a bit of money, you see. And if you wear a cardigan or two you can turn the heating off until late afternoon.

The bunker mentality remained in Roger's blood for the rest of his life – but when he passed away, his children were staggered to discover he was actually a millionaire many times over, and had a huge portfolio of stocks and bonds.

His longstanding beliefs about his inability to provide for himself and his family were deeply rooted in the mindset of scarcity. In his mind he was forevermore 'on the breadline' from the day the British Government handed out ration books. Thus he spent his entire adult life doubting whether he would be able to feed, clothe and house his own family.

Roger had the overriding sense that there wasn't enough to go around - and in a way he carried the same sense of lack as we often experience when we get ourselves in a financial pickle. Yet Roger died with enough money in the bank to stay at the Ritz for the last decade of his days on earth, ordering room-service and 'living the life of Riley'.

Don't Let Mindset Take *You* From The Ritz To The Blitz

You might be shocked to discover that since your debt problems got a bit out of hand you've actually denied yourself in a lot of ways, just like Roger. When I look at some people's debt-recovery plans laid before me, I cannot help but enquire, 'Where's the fun?'

And it's clear that – week after week – they slowly forgot how to *have* fun: 'What exactly do you mean by *fun*?' And so I ask them about the last time they had dinner at a restaurant, saw a film at the cinema, or went ten-pin bowling! You know... fun!

'You don't know what my life is *like* right now. I'm in debt up to my eyeballs. I'd just be spending another person's money...

It all has someone else's name written on it!' Well, that's a weird story to invent about what's in your wallet – about as unhelpful as it can get. If that's how it feels to you right now, then like Roger you might well have an important lesson to explore.

What Does A Millionaire Eat For Breakfast?

Of course your initial goal in applying the secret science of the 'Galatea Effect' will be to start to get yourself out of the hole; to stop living a life of scarcity and lack; to understand the power of self-expectation – no more ambitious than that.

But there is a way to feel like a *millionaire* before tomorrow's breakfast, even if you're unlikely to *realise* that goal until some years down the line. After all, if the Galatea Effect is all about 'self-fulfilling prophecies', there's nothing wrong with *experimenting* with the idea, is there? If you wanted to develop a mindset of abundance, one very good way might be to be a saver and a giver at the same time.

Andrew Reynolds, interviewed in Self-Made Millionaire *in 2008, lists his two hobbies as 'making money and giving it to charity.' Having created an extraordinarily successful business from a spare room, he is quoted as saying 'When I was young, I always promised myself that if I ever made any money, I would do something useful with it.'*

You may have heard of this concept, often in a religious context. It goes way back: Anglo-Saxon farmers were obliged to donate a tenth of their harvest each season to the Church. It was considered a duty to contribute a portion of what you received on a regular basis.

I myself don't *like* the idea of contribution being a 'duty' because it doesn't embrace what I think of as the mindset of abundance. When there's more than enough to go around, giving some of what you have has nothing to do with a sense of obligation.

Good Grief! Somebody Ate The Last Chicken Wing

Have you ever been at a barbecue when someone asks, 'Do you mind if I have that last chicken wing?' Now if you were the host, you might think to yourself, 'Good grief! How much more can he *eat*? I was going to save that for my lunch tomorrow.' But what trills out of your mouth? 'Of course. Please. Have the baked potato too… No, really.' All the while you were just doing your bit… Duty.

Suppose you thought, 'Gosh, there's plenty here. We actually could have invited the Pattersons as well.' Then you wouldn't really *care* if somebody ate the last chicken wing. This is the essence of the mindset of abundance; the belief that sits easily alongside the idea of 'contribution'. In one way or another it says, 'I trust the sense that I have enough.'

Some people contribute a portion of their *income*, some volunteer their *time*, and others share their *know-how*. If you want to do this, of course it doesn't have to be a tenth either. Whatever's appropriate and doesn't cause resentment is the right amount to give. Inherent to whatever form of contribution you make is the message that, 'There's still enough for me; I have plenty. I'm not losing out by doing this.'

Just Try To Put A Price-Tag On *That*

What is weird is that the more you give, the more it comes back in your direction. It doesn't mean that you give a fiver to a charity and 'The Universe' sends another fiver through the pipeline in another way. This flow of abundance might take another form: perhaps an increased sense of purpose and meaning... try to put a price-tag on that! Whatever you choose to give, would it be fair to say that on one level you feel abundant enough to afford to give it? Now *there's* something to think about.

It's not just a warm fuzzy feeling, either. If you believe that your life is somehow lacking, you'll be *looking out* for evidence that your particular slant on things is 'the truth', consciously or unconsciously. *That will* be your interpretation. We usually make our life's events fit the story, no matter what story we choose. People tend to get exactly what they focus on. Be careful about the stories you tell yourself.

Right now, can you afford to contribute something without resenting it? That's a decision only you can make. It's worth a try, even if you start out small. See if you get any evidence supporting my kooky idea that somehow you get more than you give.

To me, this stuff is not about percentages. It's about starting to experience the *feeling* that you've got enough, and starting to nurture a sense of self-worth through creating possibilities for other people.

What Possibilities Do *You* Want To Create?

So what possibilities do you want to create? You may want to volunteer your time. You may want to share your knowledge. If you have decided you want to contribute a bit of your income, be sure to give to something you feel passionate about. Don't contribute if you feel indifferent to what the organisation does, or how they spend their money. Remember: this isn't about duty, but it isn't about indifference either. It's about what you want to be a part of.

The best way to do this is to 'set it and forget it'; arrange for your contribution to be taken as an electronic payment on a regular basis. It makes a lot of sense, doesn't it? To keep up the pace of your sense of contribution, you've got to do it as consistently as you pay your debts. If you contribute a set amount each month, or a set amount every time you receive, the small differences go unnoticed.

If you just sort of 'see how it goes', then wait until the Festive Season every year to drop something into a bucket outside your local supermarket, you'll probably not feel the same in doing it. It might also compromise something else in your life to try to do it all at once.

A Lump Of Sourdough Can Do Its Thing For Decades

Have you ever had friends who give so much that they have no more left to give? In my circle, one such friend was Michaela. She would often pop over for a coffee, but she'd be armed with literally bags of shopping – biscuits, cakes, fruit, sugar, milk and so on. It wasn't necessary. We had all of the above. It was the most expensive cup of coffee I had ever seen anyone buy! Despite our protestations, she never came empty-handed.

And if we invited her over for a meal, we'd have enough wine, cheese and biscuits to last until December! I later learned that whenever she came over for a coffee or a meal, she would invariably spend the entire contents of her wallet. It seemed she was indeed 'generous to a fault'. But whose fault *was* it?

I became fascinated, and started to observe how Michaela behaved with other people. One Sunday afternoon someone said to her, 'I love your wristwatch. Where did you get it?' So off it came, followed by: 'No, I insist. If you really like it, then I want you to have it. I'm not so fussed about it anyway.'

Later that day, Michaela rang to ask me if I had a spare wristwatch that she could borrow to wear at the office. It seemed she had now given all of hers away – including this last one, her all-time favourite. I told her I'd be happy to oblige. But Michaela's habit of giving to excess reminded me of something from my childhood.

Centuries ago, bread bakers used to keep a live yeast culture to hand, and actually 'fed' it on a daily basis. Sourdough bread is made with such a culture, known as a 'starter'. If you've ever been to San Francisco, then you'll probably have experienced its distinctive tangy taste.

When I was a kid there was sort of a network of neighbours giving each other a cup of their prized starter to kick things off. It was truly the gift that kept on giving. Each starter was unique, but – properly cared for – a sourdough starter can do its thing for decades.

My grandmother had one of the oldest and best ones. She always kept a ball of starter under a piece of muslin in the

fridge, and we kids would walk to her house on Saturdays and ask if we could make a loaf of bread.

But there was one Golden Rule: you had to break off a piece from the ball kept in the fridge, then put the rest back. She used to say to us, 'Like a lot of things in this life, if you give away too much, there's nothing left to give. As long as I can keep enough for me, I can go on sharing with you.'

Promise You Won't Break Grandma's Golden Rule?

Isn't it so true – about *everything* – when you stop and think about it? If you give away the whole of what you've got – whether it's love, free time, money or sourdough starter – the giving stops dead in its tracks.

If, like Michaela, you've forgotten how important it is to save enough for yourself so you can keep on sharing, you're not fully embracing the mindset of abundance. When that is the case, you soon find debt repayment and wealth creation a struggle – and eventually you resent what you're doing.

You feel abundant if you know you've got enough. You can feel abundant *today* if your story about yourself is that there is always enough for you – and maybe a bit left over, too. If this particular lesson is one you grapple with whenever you lick the stamp to send off a payment for your credit card bill, stop for an hour or two, put your calculator away, and go ten-pin bowling immediately. Spend some money on yourself! And be sure to invite a friend or two along – *your* treat, by the way!

Never A Better Time To Road-Test Your New Life

I believe that – for each and every one of us – the path we're meant to follow is in our sightlines the entire way, if we just took a moment to look. Even if we lose our bearings from time to time, the path is *there* somewhere. But if it still feels as if you're starting off by driving in the dark, remember... you'll soon see the dawn. Gone will be the days of being asleep at the wheel. Gone will be the days of being lost and directionless. Instead you'll be on the way toward achieving *your* definition of prosperity, freedom and abundance.

Look ahead to the horizon. What do you see? All your debts behind you? A bit of money in the bank? A new-found sense of purpose and meaning? A life in financial control? The resulting sense of freedom all this mastery brings?

Wealth isn't just a matter of how big your personal pile of poker chips is. But whatever you decide 'wealth' means to you, don't be a passenger. Get in the front seat. Take control of the steering wheel, and travel wherever you want to go.

True freedom lies ahead, if you *choose* it. Your particular dreams and aspirations are unique. Just like everyone else, you deserve to see more of what's possible out there. My very best wishes go out to you.

Sadly, my Grandpa Jack passed on a few years ago, joining others who were special teachers to me during their time on this planet. I often miss his pragmatism and the generosity behind his particular brand of humour.

With the passing of friends and family, I remind myself that when we go wherever we go, we try to leave a piece of ourselves behind with someone we knew – and not just in a silver urn. Somewhere along the way, we can help shape another person's character… and that's the most meaningful contribution any of us can make by a long shot.

If you've been inspired by this book, I'd love to hear how and why – and would consider it a gift. By all means share your doubts and fears – but please share your successes and achievements as well. You can reach me at **www. wealthmechanic.com/inspired**.

This can be the year that you begin to realise your dreams, so do your best to expand your horizons. Tap into the secret science of the 'Galatea Effect' as if your very future depends on it… because it probably *does*. Expect great things to happen and work toward bringing them to fruition.

You already have everything you need so just sit back, relax, and enjoy the ride – but get a move on, won't you? It's never too late to be what you might have been.

THE NUTS AND BOLTS OF THIS SECTION

☞ The right mental attitude *alone* can often bring abundance into your life

☞ If you want to develop a mindset of abundance, a good way is through making a contribution

☞ Doing things for others can do quite a lot for you. The more you give, the more it comes back

☞ Never give so much that you have no more left to give. If you give away all you've got, the giving stops

☞ Wealth isn't just a matter of how big your pile of poker chips is; it is largely measured in the mind

Some Of The Other Forms Of 'Breakdown Assistance'

Below is a list of specialised debt agencies and related resources in the UK whose details were correct at the time of going to press. Most countries have similar agencies, either nationally or (especially in North America) locally. Details of your nearest point-of-resource are readily available online.

Citizens Advice Bureau (CAB): Association offering free, independent and confidential face-to-face debt advice that can be accessed through 3,400 service-outlets throughout England and Wales. Locate your nearest outlet through the telephone directory or online.

Telephone: local listings regionally

Website: www.adviceguide.org.uk

Consumer Credit Counselling Service (CCCS): Registered charity offering free, independent and confidential advice, counselling and repayment plans. It can help you prioritise debts and will often liaise with creditor on your behalf.

Telephone: 0800-138-1111

Website: www.cccs.co.uk

Credit Action: Money-education charity committed to helping people manage their money better and stay in control. It provides advocacy, collaboration and partnerships with various organisations.

Telephone: 01522-699-777

Website: www.creditaction.co.uk

Email: office@creditaction.co.uk

Debtors Anonymous: Fellowship programme for both compulsive debtors and under-earners who desire to stop incurring unsecured debt. It includes a distinct but not separate programme called Business Debtors Anonymous.

Telephone: 020-7644-5070

Website: www.debtorsanonymous.org.uk

Email: info@debtorsanonymous.org.uk

Gamcare: Registered charity dedicated to addressing the social impact of gambling and assisting persons adversely affected by it. It provides practical advice to problem gamblers, which includes resources on debt.

Telephone: 0845-6000-133

Website: www.gamcare.org.uk

Email: info@gamcare.org.uk

National Debtline: Telephone-based service offering free, independent and confidential advice and self-help information packs to those in debt.

Telephone: 0808-808-4000

Website: www.nationaldebtline.co.uk

Payplan: Debt-management company financed by the credit industry, providing free, independent and confidential debt advice and support. Services range from providing simple budgeting and income-maximisation advice to longer-term debt solutions.

Telephone: 0800-716-239

Website: www.payplan.com

Email: help@payplan.com

UK Insolvency Helpline: Online resource with telephone advice for those in debt.
It may be of particular interest to limited companies, sole traders and business partnerships, as well as those struggling with student debt.

Telephone: 0800-074-6918

Website: www.insolvencyhelpline.co.uk

Email: info@insolvencyehelpline.co.uk

Additional resources are available at *www.wealthmechanic.com/resources* or online

Wealth Success Strategies Masterclass:

A Special Bonus Opportunity from North Star Press Ltd (Exclusively for our Readers)

As a way of saying thanks for purchasing *Under The Hood*, Max Eames has agreed to offer you free access to a set of home learning masterclasses.* Yes, you and a family member can both attend as complimentary guests. The normal charge for this opportunity to kick-start your long-forgotten dreams is £100 (that's $200) per participant – but because you have purchased the book, you and your chosen guest can participate for the cost of a friendly phone call.

Guest admission passes are available to purchasers of this book, but access is on a first-come-first-served basis, and spaces are often limited. To assure access to the next available *Wealth Success Strategies* masterclass, please register immediately on **www.wealthsuccessstrategies.com/guest**. By taking full advantage of this no obligation gift, you will be able to expand on the insights provided in this book by discovering:

- A set of 3 rarely-understood enhancements to your debt-elimination (and later wealth-creation) strategies

- How to release your unconscious emotional 'roadblocks', the single most common set of barriers to lasting financial freedom for most of the people you know

- A powerful list of questions that will unravel even the most entrenched set of behaviours that, unchecked, will hold you back and prevent your progress

- The one and only thing out there that is guaranteed to obliterate feelings of fear, doubt and shame forever

- How to get the most mileage out of the world's easiest and most effective debt-recovery methods with no more than a calculator by your side

- A simple 3-step exercise you can do at home to give yourself what it takes to bring positive changes into your life, starting tomorrow

There is only one condition: that you have at least familiarised yourself with the contents of this book before you enrol. This way, by the time you participate in the *Wealth Success Strategies* masterclass, you will have explored a set of understandings that will not only bring you financial freedom down the line, but will develop your sense of genuine happiness at the same time.

If you believe you've been forever hovering below your full potential – be that in terms of your income, your bank balance, or your sense of enjoyment out of life – then register for the masterclass as though your very future depended on it (but note that, because of the usual ticket price of this opportunity, it is necessary to use the following VIP passcode for readers to gain access to the registration area: WM27).

*This offer is available to all readers of *Under The Hood* by Max Eames. The offer itself is limited to the *Wealth Success Strategies* masterclass only, and access is subject to availability and changes to programme schedule. Participants in the masterclass are under no additional financial obligation whatsoever, either to North Star Press Ltd or to Max Eames. North Star Group Ltd reserves the right to withhold access to anyone it believes would adversely affect the participation and enjoyment of others, and to revoke access at any time to anyone it believes is disrupting the home learning opportunity for other participants.

ABOUT THE AUTHOR

About Max Eames

Max Eames grew up in California, but settled in the United Kingdom after completing an honours degree in Florence, Italy. His varied career has included work as a chartered architect and a restaurateur.

A London-based psychotherapist, he facilitates long-lasting personal transformations for those who recognise the need to challenge both self-defeating behaviours and self-limiting beliefs.

About Under The Hood

Your struggle with money usually has more to do with what's 'under the hood' (in other words, your personal psychology) than what's in your wallet. So if you seem to be 'cash-strapped' month after month, this book aims to help you figure out why.

Under The Hood will give you an understanding of why it's often so hard, despite our best intentions, to keep our hands in our pockets and our money in our wallets. Then you'll gain powerful insights into who you are as a person, as well as *strategies* you can use to turn your beliefs and values to best advantage.

Finally, you'll master the secret science of the Galatea Effect so it works *for* you, not against you. Use this simple psychology to transform your bank balance, and then apply it to the rest of your life. Whether you want to make changes in relation to your job, your relationships, or your lifestyle, it will set the wheels in motion for *lasting* results.

Author photograph by Gaz, www.pgb-portraits.com

About Fix Your Finances

When it comes to money management, nothing just 'happens' by itself: if you don't have a get-out-of-debt-and-stay-out plan, somebody will have a get-into-debt-and-stay-there plan to torment you with. There's always *some* sort of strategy or plan at work – either yours or somebody else's.

This book is the logical companion to *Under The Hood*: once you've understood the 'psychology' of debt, you'll no doubt be eager for some debt-elimination 'technology' that really *works*.

In *Fix Your Finances,* you'll be armed with every tool you need to rapidly increase your debt repayments – and to build up a comfortable cash reserve, maybe for the first time ever.

Requiring only a few minutes to get things firing on all cylinders, each section contains a combination of practical insights, true-life stories and step-by-step activities that can lead *you* out of debt quickly and forever.

About The Wealth Mechanic Programme

The *Wealth Mechanic* programme has proven to be a hyper-speed escape route for countless families and individuals. And it might well be the surest, simplest and most practical way for *you* to get out of debt and *stay* out forever – without the slightest risk of destroying your credit rating or tarnishing your good name.

Wealth Mechanic offers the opportunity for a fresh start, a chance to 'repair the engine' and calibrate it to your own specifications. Combining the material from *Under The Hood* and *Fix Your Finances* into one convenient volume, this book structures it into a straightforward 31-day action plan that you can follow at your own pace and in your own spare time.

Lightning Source UK Ltd.
Milton Keynes UK
22 September 2009
144008UK00001B/14/P